A THEOLOGY
OF THE DARK SIDE

PUTTING THE POWER OF EVIL IN ITS PLACE

Nigel Goring Wright

InterVarsity Press
Downers Grove, Illinois

InterVarsity Press
P.O. Box 1400, Downers Grove, IL 60515-1426
Internet: www.ivpress.com
E-mail: mail@ivpress.com

InterVarsity Press® is the book-publishing division of InterVarsity Christian Fellowship/USA®, a student movement active on campus at hundreds of universities, colleges and schools of nursing in the United States of America, and a member movement of the International Fellowship of Evangelical Students. For information about local and regional activities, write Public Relations Dept., InterVarsity Christian Fellowship/USA, 6400 Schroeder Rd., P.O. Box 7895, Madison, WI 53707-7895, or visit the IVCF website at <www.intervarsity.org>.

Cover design: Cindy Kiple

Cover image: Erich Lessing/Art Resource, NY

ISBN 0-8308-2789-7

Printed in the United States of America ∞

Library of Congress Cataloging-in-Publication Data

Wright, Nigel, 1949-
    A theology of the dark side: putting the power of evil in its
    place/Nigel Goring Wright.
        p. cm.
    Includes bibliographical references.
    ISBN 0-8308-2789-7 (pbk.: alk. paper)
    1. Theodicy. 2. Good and evil. I. Title
    BT160.W75 2004
    231'.8—dc22

                                                                    2004008464

P	19	18	17	16	15	14	13	12	11	10	9	8	7	6	5	4	3	2	1
Y	18	18	17	16	15	14	13	12	11	10	09	08	07	06	05	04				

After 911, people condemned God —

Dedicated with affection and respect
to the pastors and churches of "Mainstream North"

CONTENTS

PREFACE

Of the various books I have written, that titled *The Fair Face of Evil: Putting the Power of Darkness in its Place*[1] is probably the one people ask after most. Sadly the book has been out of print for some years. Paternoster Press was kind enough to inquire about whether I would be willing to have it be reprinted. This seemed a good idea except for two things. First, the illustrations and references in the book are now dated. Although I saw no reason why they should be removed, I did see they could be complemented to provide a more contemporary feel. Second, over the years I have thought further and read more about the subject matter of the book. For some time I had been contemplating an article that might take my train of thought further concerning the "nature" of evil and could give an account of how my mind has changed. I might still do this by way of a focused summary, but I also welcome the opportunity to rewrite the original book and to develop its analyses and proposals. The book you now hold is the product of this rewriting. Its title is different, not as a way of ensnaring unwary readers into purchasing a book they may already possess but as a way of signifying its status as a reworked and rewritten contribution to debate. Even those who possess the original may be interested in revisiting, as I have done, its ideas and perspectives.

Things have, of course, moved on. Demons are no longer the hot topic they were in the 1980s and 1990s, and for that we breathe a sigh of relief. Belief frenzies are as unhelpful as any other frenzy. "Territorial spirits" have also enjoyed some exposure and are, I suspect, still hanging around as a topic at least for the time being. The underlying issues about the nature of evil will, however, never go away. They are perennial and those who are believers in the God of Jesus Christ need to be well armed both intellectually and spiritually to address them. Above all, this book is about how we are to *think* about evil and by derivation how we are *not* to think. I could not agree more with Walter Wink when he says, "One of the most pressing questions facing the world today is, How can we oppose evil without creating new evils and being made evil ourselves?"[2] In this I reveal my conviction, as a theologian, that getting our ways of thinking and believing right (or as right as we can) is part of the process of getting our ways of living and acting right. It works the other way around as well. Right thinking does not mean having an answer for everything but knowing the limits of what we can know, or should know, and developing models to guide our action. It will be clear at points in this book that I have reached my limits and also that I am willing to admit areas of unresolved tension in the proposals I advance. I hope that if it ever came down to it I might be willing to go to the stake for belief in the triune God. I feel quite differently of how we think about evil. The devil is not a confessional issue. This book is sometimes speculative and often tentative. It is an exploration and I might find, given further years of thought, that I would not wish to be held to its constructs. I hope it might however stimulate our corporate thinking as the church of God.

The title of the first British version of this work, *The Fair Face of Evil*, excited both amusement and puzzlement. Since it appeared immediately above my name some drew the obvious inference. Others found it somewhat opaque and enigmatic. Interestingly, a book has recently appeared out of a very different stable from the one I represent but with a title that is not so far from what I was wanting. *Lure of the Sinister*[3] captures that sense of attraction to the dark and murky about which I was writing and to which even Christians can fall prey. Indeed, is it Christians *in particular* who fall prey—precisely because they are so swift to identify and then, righteously, to combat what is evil that they run ahead of where common and theological sense ought to lead them? If Gareth Medway, a pagan and priest of Themis in the Fellowship of Isis (so he tells us),[4] is to be believed, Christians end up inventing things that do not exist. So faith lapses into gullibility.

I cannot pretend that I do not believe this sometimes happens, although it ought to be abundantly clear I also think there is more to it than that. The title of the first American edition of this book, and of the first chapter of this present one, with its reference to a "Satan syndrome" makes this pathological possibility clear. How we think things through might help us avoid the distortions that, so to speak, give Satan, and sometimes Christians, a bad name.

CHAPTER ONE

THE SATAN SYNDROME

The interview took place in the Museum of Childhood, Bethnal Green, London. It was the early 1990s and much excitement was being caused by the phenomenon of satanic ritual abuse.[1] People were claiming that it was widespread. American social workers and law enforcement officers had started it all off, and the cause was being taken up by a number of Christians. Eventually a government-sponsored inquiry concluded there was nothing to it.[2] In the meantime, however, there was a spirited debate about the nature and existence of evil. I had written around this topic, and the researchers were on to me. Joan Bakewell, on behalf of the TV program *Heart of the Matter*, asked me the significant question, What is the difference between something being "wrong" and something being "evil"?

It is a good question. We could say that there is a point at which the quantitative becomes qualitative: a great quantity of wrong actions crosses a threshold, gains a dynamic and acquires an identity that produces the quality of evilness. We could argue that, with some people, at some times, there is such a huge loss of the *humanum*, an evacuation of simple humaneness, that they enter into a different plane, which we call evil.

All of us may imagine ourselves doing wrong things, but equally, for all of us, there are actions that are just so unimaginable, so bereft of kindness, that we find nothing good or mitigating to say in the face of them: the planning and execution of the Nazi death camps; the murder of an innocent and helpless child; the piloting of aircraft into the World Trade

Center; the reptilian conduct that leads to the massacres of ethnic cleansing; the systematic killing by a general practitioner of his own patients. We think ourselves to be in a different league and designate such actions as evil.

There is no reason why Christians should not follow this approach. But they have wanted throughout history to give more substance to evil. Without necessarily following it, I appreciate the perspective that Walter Brueggemann brings to this issue. God created and ordered a world out of the chaos, which according to Genesis 1:1-2 was "formless and void." In the biblical story that follows, it seems that chaos persists. God's ordered creation is therefore continually threatened by a powerful and effective adversary. The powers of negation and death loose in the world are never quite overcome by Yahweh, and they exist to resist and nullify creation. The chaos makes incursions into God's creation, occasionally using historical agents to do so.[3] This sense of a powerful adversary becomes sharpened and honed in the New Testament. It exists in the world as an objective reality, as the devil, or Satan, or the "prince of this world." This book is an exploration of what this language means.

In the first major work of systematic theology in the church's history, it was already recognized that *how* the devil and demons exist and *what* they are is an open space for theological exploration, even if decided opinions are held by some.

> In regard to the devil and his angels and the opposing spiritual powers, the Church teaching lays it down that these beings exist, but what or how they are or how they exist it has not been explained very clearly. Amongst many Christians, however, the following opinion is held, that this devil was formerly an angel, but became an apostate and persuaded as many angels as he could to fall away with him.[4]

In recent years, after a period of apparent seclusion and retirement, the devil is back in business. Of course, some people know that he's never really been out of it. Like Voldemort in the Harry Potter books, his disappearance from the scene was distinctly temporary, a time of gathering strength for a greater onslaught.

In the world and in the church we are inclined to approach the devil with newfound respect or even fascination. Some of the old certainties have become muted. The rationalism that came to expression in the eighteenth-century Enlightenment had little room for the idea of demons. Reacting to the dominant influence of generations of church theology, the balance shifted from reliance on the authority of traditions or Scripture toward an emphasis on the rational capacity of the human mind. The principle of doubt became significant in the quest for knowledge. Thinkers were no longer convinced about the validity of metaphysical speculation. Humankind's proper concern was conceived to be the objective, empirical world about which reasonable and verifiable statements could be made. Blaming the devil for things that could not easily be explained came to be seen as superstition—and dangerous superstition at that. The scientific revolution that was under way encouraged people to believe that everything could be explained by reference to natural processes and that, at least in principle, one day this process would be complete. Mysteries would yield to science. Where does the devil fit into this increasingly unmysterious world? Come to think of it, where does God fit?

No one in his or her right mind would want to put the clock back three hundred years. The scientific, intellectual and industrial revolutions that shape our modern world have brought immense benefits. We might think, for example, of the material benefits that have delivered so many in the Western world from want and drudgery and have brought marvelous new possibilities within the reach of ordinary people. By and large we live longer and better because of the Enlightenment revolution in our understanding of ourselves and of our environment.

But other benefits are not so immediately obvious to us. It is at least arguable that the Enlightenment effected a deliverance from superstition, which has set subsequent generations free from neurotic and paranoid fears of some kind of cosmic plot. For reasons buried deep in human psychology, the mind easily embraces conspiracy theories. The world is a far simpler place if we identify the enemy and project all our fears and doubts onto him, her, it or them. If I can attribute the rot in my society to the subversive influence (say) of communist infiltrators then I have some sort of framework for living and acting in the world. If I am able to identify some agents (it used to be the Soviets but is now more likely to be nations sponsoring terrorism) as the focus of evil in the modern world, then it makes it easier to decide what I must do. If, as in Nazi Germany, the ills of society can be blamed on the Jews, then life's complex decisions become much easier since somebody else is to blame and not me. For some it is people of religious faith who constitute the threat, with belief in God being the source of all evil. These conspiracy theories find a ready audience in our human mind.

For many in pre-Enlightenment Europe belief in the devil amounted to a conspiracy theory writ large. The paranoid worldview was in vogue. It has been estimated that 100,000 people may have perished between 1450 and 1700 in what has been called "the great witch craze." This was a movement that had its roots in the Inquisition, the medieval tribunal that attempted to eradicate heresy and witchcraft by the use of torture and executions.

The climate of opinion that developed held that a cosmic plot directed by Satan threatened all Christian society. In Catholic and Protestant territories alike "millions were persecuted and tens of millions terrified and intimidated during one of the longest and strangest delusions in history."[5] The disturbing point to note is that such a craze could probably only have developed in areas where people looked at the world from a Judaeo-Christian-Islamic point of view. It was the Enlightenment that put an end to the witch craze. Its reasoned and scientific approach to life had no room for witchcraft. In the light of the facts it is difficult to regret this.

It is not, therefore, surprising that Satan has experienced an eclipse in the consciousness of most Western people for the last several hundred years. According to Walter Wink, angels, demons and the devil have become the unmentionables of our society, the "drunk uncle" that people would rather forget about. In

> "sophisticated" circles accounts of sexual exploits scarcely raise an eyebrow, but if you want to bring all talk to a halt in shocked embarrassment, every eye riveted on you, try mentioning angels, or demons, or the devil. You will quickly be appraised for signs of pathological violence and then quietly shunned.[6]

The devil has come to be seen in society and in the church as a piece of mythological baggage that belongs to a previous and outdated worldview.

With only sense, experience and reason to go on, and with no rational place for an evil "first cause," enlightened people simply dropped the devil from consideration. With direct psychic experience no longer admissible as evidence of his reality, the devil was as good as dead.[7] While, among thinking people, the devil was being reinterpreted as the external projection of humankind's own internal demons, the church also felt the force of the problem.

The intellectual revolutions of the eighteenth century raised the question (one that is still with us) of how literally we are to understand the Bible. If we now no longer accept the (supposed) biblical worldview of a three-story universe, why should we continue to believe in the devil? So the devil became a candidate for demythologizing. Rudolf Bultmann spoke, and speaks, for many when he wrote these often quoted words, "No-one can use the electric light and the radio or the discoveries of modern medicine and at the same time believe in the New Testament world of spirits and miracles."[8]

Few theologians argue that the New Testament references to the devil are meaningless, but the majority would argue that they need to be reinterpreted for a scientific age. So it is that the "demons" of the Gospels are to be understood as the primitive descriptions of afflictions now treated by physicians and psychiatrists, while the "principalities and powers" of Paul's letters are said to correspond to the concerns of present-day politicians and sociologists.[9] The clear implication is that the notion of the devil and of demons is no longer necessary in our world. The devil has passed his sell-by date. His services are no longer required. Yet, dead though he may be, the devil refuses to lie down. Even in scientific, technological societies such as our own there is a resurgence of interest in the devil, which can be seen in a number of ways.

THE INADEQUACY OF MATERIALISM

It seems that humankind is not satisfied with purely materialistic explanations of human existence. There is a certain kind of scientist strongly motivated to see the scientific method made absolute—the way of explaining, and explaining away, the religious dimension of life. The suspicion is that such people are motivated more by an ideology than by science itself. They have decided what the answer should be and have no difficulty thereafter in finding it. But human experience cannot be reduced to purely scientific categories, and there have consistently been reactions against attempts to do this. It is as though people need to subvert the scientism that is in danger of absolutizing itself and enthroning its practitioners as the new high priests of reality.

The Enlightenment was followed by the Romantic movement, a revolt against merely rational explanations of life that took no account of the mysterious and mystical dimensions of human experience. Romanticism found great depths and heights in the beauties of nature, literature and music, which were seen as testimonies to the supernatural capacities of human beings. A radio interview in 1985 with the lawyer and novelist John Mortimer, long known for his atheism, revealed a similar tendency.[10] Mortimer spoke of his increasing interest in religion, of his recognition of the need for a mystical aspect to life and of the fact that he believed everything about Christianity except for the existence of God!

Though there has been a decline in Christian faith in our own culture, there has not necessarily been a decline in religion. Though less Christian, people are not necessarily less religious. G. K. Chesterton was accurate when he claimed that those who cease believing in Christianity do not believe in nothing—they will believe in anything. Other forms of religious expression have moved into the space left unoccupied by Christianity. Religion has mutated rather than disappeared. Many of these new forms of religion may be described as secular religions, or even as idolatries. But they testify to the fact that humankind is incurably religious or, as somebody has said, *"homo sapiens* is *ipso facto homo religiosus"*: human beings are intrinsically religious.[11]

Remarkably, despite years of secularizing influence, there still arises in human beings the desire for nonmaterialistic perspectives on life. This may help to explain why it is that language about God and the devil continues to have currency in our own culture. Although people have difficulty with the thought of God or the devil, something about human experience finds expression in this way and not adequately in any other way. The use of this language (outdated though it may seem) thus "allows us to reclaim, name and comprehend types of experience that materialism renders mute and inexpressible."[12]

The world is far more mysterious a place than the purely materialistic understanding of it would lead us to suppose. Paradoxically it is the ongoing march of science that is increasingly confirming the basic human instinct that seeks for spiritual fulfillment. Science, far from reducing reality to simple formulae, displays its complexities and mysteries.

THE EXPERIENCE OF THE TWENTIETH CENTURY

There is a further factor that explains the enduring usefulness of "diabolical" language. The twentieth century opened with a sense of hope and optimism about the perfectibility and progress of humankind. The carnage of the Great War and the unspeakable blasphemies of the Nazi era and the Second World War have left us in a far more chastened mood. The events of the Third Reich are hard to describe in ordinary language. How can we account for the way in which one of the most advanced nations on earth became, for all intents and purposes, demonized? Or what manner of forces could produce the horror of the Holocaust?

The events of that period continue to appall, fascinate and elude subsequent generations as we still come to terms with the horrific magnitude of it all. To quote Emil Brunner:

> A generation which has produced two world wars, and a totalitarian state with all its horrors, has very little cause to designate the Middle Ages as "dark." . . . On the contrary it is just because our generation has experienced such diabolical wickedness that many people have abandoned their former "enlightened" objection to the existence of a "power of darkness," and are now prepared to believe in Satan as represented in the Bible.[13]

In response to such experiences theologians have reflected again on the nature of the demonic. In the face of actual experience it becomes increasingly necessary to bring the devil back from retirement and press him into service again.

The Second World War is only the tip of the iceberg. Increasingly, while psychology has opened up the drives and impulses that unconsciously shape human beings, sociology has opened up the reality of suprapersonal forces that shape human societies. Humankind is not completely the master of its own fate but is held by a network of social, political, economic and cultural forces, which make it what it is. When confronted by the divided communities of Northern Ireland, the intractable conflict between Israelis and Palestinians, the deprived and exploited areas of the Third World, the impersonal capitalism of multinational companies, we search for language to describe the suprahuman powers that are at work and are pushed toward the category of the demonic.

THE GROWTH OF OCCULTISM

Almost forty years ago a writer on the subject clearly envisaged that witchcraft would continue its rapid dying process in the face of "the popular press, popular education, a national health scheme, and the American Way of Life"![14] Clearly at that time there was little indication of the explosion in occult interest that has taken place since. It is not my intention to chart this explosion since others have written more than enough on the subject already.[15] We simply register here the growth of interest in the paranormal in recent decades and seek a perspective on it. It may be helpful to distinguish four aspects of such interest.

Scientific interest. Since human claims to be affected by an invisible world of reality that interacts with the visible world are widespread and persistent, scientists have begun to regard this as an area of legitimate investigation. This inquiry is sometimes called "parapsychology," and there is now in Britain at least one university chair in the subject (at Edinburgh University). As a scientific discipline it has yet to gain the acceptance and respect of other disciplines. This nonacceptance is because parapsychology is unable to prove itself within the accepted canons of scientific research.

Psi (the hypothetical energy force that is under investigation) and the psychic phenomena it produces tend to be somewhat elusive. After nearly fifty years of research, parapsychology has arguably little to show by way of assured results besides the conclusion (based on experiments in statistical probability) that some forms of extrasensory perception seem possible.[16]

Of course, the lack of assured results may itself be because there is a dimension of reality at work here that is not subject to the ordinary methods of the material or behavioral sciences. As Christians claim the same for the experience of knowing God, or prayer, maybe other aspects of human experience cannot be analyzed by science in its current state of understanding or with its present methodologies. Still, with whatever degree of success, recent years have seen the attempt to take seriously that dimension of experience we call the "paranormal," and this has lent a degree of acceptability to the subject.

Human interest. Whatever science may or may not be able to prove makes little difference to those large sections of the human race that take it for granted that humans possess "psychic powers." *The X-Files* has been one of the most successful of recent TV programs and has highlighted this interest. Much of what is called the occult is simply exploration of the inner world of human consciousness.

It is commonly accepted that the conscious mind is only the tip of the iceberg that is the human psyche. There are vast, uncharted regions that belong to the individual unconscious and even, as C. G. Jung argued, the "racial" unconscious. (We will refer to this at several points in this book.) In the subconscious regions there are potentialities and possibilities that surprise the conscious mind and give rise to unusual phenomena, perceptions, trance-like states, healing abilities, religious emotions and ecstatic conditions without the need to refer either to the devil or to God by way of direct explanation. These are simply testimonies to the fertile and productive nature of the subconscious mind.

Michael Perry in the book *Deliverance*, produced by the Christian Exorcism Study Group, finds it possible to understand a range of psychic phenomena without recourse to the devil or demons. Poltergeists, for instance, are not essentially evil or malevolent entities but rather projections into the environment of psychic energy resulting from stressful situations. The right Christian response to these phenomena is not exorcism but ministry to the situation of conflict and the formal blessing of individuals to restore peace.[17]

Similarly, ghosts are not invariably the product of evil forces, but "place memories," imprints left on the environment by repetitive or emotion-laden past events that are picked up in the present by a receptive individual.[18] Spiritualism is not necessarily occult activity but "a cult based on a somewhat credulous approach to highly selective aspects of paranormal phenomena."[19]

Perry's book is noteworthy for its judicious and balanced approach and for two further characteristics. First, despite the lack of scientific "proof," Perry and the group he represents accept paranormal phenomena as part of the totality of human experience that, although not scientifically susceptible to categorization, can be reflected on and described as real experiences. Second, the book attributes much paranormal activity neither directly to God nor the devil but to the human psyche. This is not to encourage or approve it, but we need not see the devil in everything that escapes immediate comprehension or does not fit into a Christian framework.

Religious interest. Occult activity does not necessarily imply an interest in Satan. The word *occult* means "hidden," and the self-perception of most modern-day occultists is that they are exploring a form of nature religion rather than making contact with the devil. Hence witchcraft sees itself as a revival of ancient paganism and of hidden knowledge about the nature and workings of the world. The powers of nature may be used by witches, in this understanding, for both good and evil purposes.[20] Evil spirits are acknowledged, but as a danger to be resisted, not as allies to be embraced.

For occultists, therefore, the motivation is an essentially religious one: witchcraft is a way of tapping into and being at one with the benevolent forces of nature. It is the search for harmony and cooperation with the environment on which we depend. Christianity is seen as an intolerant religion, preoccupied with history rather than nature, that destroyed the ancient and indigenous religions and imposed a totalitarian ideology on an otherwise easygoing, tolerant and pleasure-seeking (rather than power-seeking) nature mysticism. This theme is coming increasingly to the fore in modern debate, not least in popular novels such as *Chocolat* by Joanne Harris.[21]

Satanic interest. A further strand of interest is specifically to do with the worship and service of Satan. Whereas witchcraft is essentially pre-Christian in its understanding of the supernatural world, Satanism, to the degree that it exists, is explicitly anti-Christian.[22] Satan is acknowledged as the ruler of the world and as son of God. The church is hated and feared. Its ceremonies are parodied and despised. There is conscious antagonism toward Christians. Satanist groups are said to be organized, disciplined and active in recruiting, but how large or widespread they are is a matter of conjecture. In the nature of the case not much is known about them, and in the absence of knowledge imagination can fill the gaps.

This description of the strands in the explosion of occult interest shows the variety of concerns at work. The power of darkness should not be regarded as equally or necessarily at work in every aspect of it. This is obviously true in regard to the scientific strand.

THE GROWTH OF THE CHARISMATIC MOVEMENT

A further reason for the resurgence of interest in the devil is the growth of the charismatic renewal movement. This has led to greater awareness of the power of God and, conversely, of the power of darkness. In charismatic groups spiritual warfare is commonly stressed. It grew first out of experiences that have come unsought after and from which a strange kind of knowledge has been derived. More cynically, it might be said that a "born-again" army requires for its justification a "born-again" enemy. The earlier awareness of the ability of demons to afflict people has developed more recently into a concept of spiritual battle for the structures and well-being of society. These issues will be examined in their place.[23] It is sufficient at the moment to stress that this book emerges from specific understandings of the power of darkness, understandings that will be most helpful in renewing the life and mission of the church of God. These healthy understandings will keep our practice healthy.

The renewal of the deliverance ministry, which has been a significant if secondary aspect of charismatic renewal, reflects the ministry of Jesus. The Son of God came into the world to destroy the works of the devil (1 Jn 3:8). The ministry of Jesus was distinctly characterized by the power to set people free from the powers of darkness (Lk 11:20). He gave his disciples authority to do the same and, when they used it, declared that he saw Satan fall like lightning from heaven (Lk 10:17-19). Jesus was an exorcist and any version of him that edits out this fact is a distorted one. The ministry of deliverance should therefore be characteristic of Christ's people, and indeed for most of its history has been just this. But it would be foolish not to recognize that there are dangers. All warfare involves danger, and in this sphere of ministry there are several dangers that lie ready at hand.

The pastoral dangers. The potential to harm individuals seeking help in this area is considerable. By wrong diagnosis and failure to discern the activity of evil influences we may end up with a superficial diagnosis that does not reach the real cause of the problem. Equally, to diagnose demons where demons do not exist and to engage in exorcism where some other form of pastoral care and healing is needed may cause unnecessary distress. It is worrying when immature and irresponsible people attempt ministry for which they are not equipped. The disciples of Jesus were hardly professionals, but it could be said of them that they had been learning from the One who was more than able to cope and were far from being novices.

The practice in the more established churches of appointing properly recognized and trained individuals working in this area, along with doctors and psychiatrists, has much to commend it. Unfortunately, good sound practices of this kind are not so easy to establish in churches of a freer faith and order. Much concern was generated quite rightly after the tragic case of the Barnsley exorcism trial in 1975 England when a man murdered his wife after an all-night exorcism. Having been told by his local vicar that he was possessed by forty demons, a group of charismatic Christians claimed to have exorcised many demons but had failed to expel the demon of murder.[24]

This case is a permanent reminder of the pastoral dangers and warns us about the need for thought-out practices and trained workers in the deliverance field. Regrettably this incident is not isolated. Other exorcists, both Christian and Muslim, have been up before the courts. We find further cause for worry against the backdrop of eight-year-old Victoria Climbié's tragic murder at the hands of her great aunt Marie Therese Kouao and her boyfriend, Carl Manning. Some of the three churches with which Victoria was peripherally connected are said to have reinforced the belief that her abused condition was a sign not of misuse at the hand of adults but of demon possession. It is claimed they practiced deliverance on her. When a documentary titled *The Possessed* was screened on May 10, 2002, it accused black-led churches of casting out demons from children as young as five. The claim met with a storm of protest from black leaders who believed they were being stereotyped.[25]

The personal dangers. The personal dangers should not be underestimated. I refer not to the dangers of temptation and spiritual assault involved in deliverance ministry but to the possibilities of being deceived and caught up in something that may push us in directions we do not wish to go. Two examples reinforce this point.

In 1980 a preacher and his friend tried to exorcise the "spirit of Judas Iscariot" from a mentally unstable woman and unintentionally killed her by jumping up and down on her body. The judge at the trial acknowledged that they had acted with honorable motives.[26] Here the warning is both of the pastoral danger and the personal danger of becoming involved with malevolent entities to such a degree that their nature inadvertently rubs off on the helper so that she becomes a little demonic herself.

In any kind of warfare the temptation is to become like the enemy—it is one of the things the dynamic of warfare does. A further example concerns the case of Derry Knight, who was found guilty at Maidstone Crown Court, England, in 1986 of obtaining over $348,500 by false pretenses from a group of Christians, whom he persuaded that he was able to buy Satanic regalia and thereby destroy a Satanic organization from within.[27] The danger present here is not of becoming demonic but of being gullible. The Satanic realm is a happy hunting ground for con artists. For those who accept the reality of the power of darkness it is possible to be drawn into a world that has its own form of plausibility but that cannot, for the most part, be verified. The possibilities of credulity are enormous. It becomes difficult to disentangle fact from fantasy.[28] How do we distinguish between the real and sinister world of darkness and plain fantasy when Christians are by definition outside it? What level of verification should be insisted on and at what points? It is possible to lose a proper sense of judgment and, by a credulous attitude, masquerading as a kind of spiritual gnosticism, give to the power of darkness more power than it possesses. This is where we come to the third danger area, the most crucial of all.

The theological dangers. These are the main concern of this book. Others have written what needs to be said pastorally. The theological issue was eloquently and classically stated by C. S. Lewis in the preface to *The Screwtape Letters*, first published in 1942:

> There are two equal and opposite errors into which our race can fall about the devils. One is to disbelieve in their existence. The other is to believe, and to feel an excessive and unhealthy interest in them. They themselves are equally pleased by both errors and hail a materialist or a magician with the same delight.[29]

Lewis puts his finger on the issue. That these words are so frequently quoted suggests he was on to something with which many have resonated. It is wrong to reject the existence of the powers of darkness, but it is equally wrong to believe in them *in the wrong way*. The rest of this book is a sustained reflection on this theme. It is precisely because the renewal movement has been in danger of falling into the second of these errors that yet another book may be necessary. How may we take the power of darkness seriously without taking it too seriously? The failure of Christians to get this right concerns me as I write. The quotation from Lewis is often used by Christian writers or speakers to warn Christians against an excessive interest in the power of darkness. The point is not that Christians aim to do this. It has to do with the "lure of the sinister." Our ways of thinking and speaking (in short, our theology) leave us giving more respect to the devil than we should ever do.

At the beginning of *The Screwtape Letters* Lewis includes a quotation from Martin Luther: "The best way to drive out the devil, if he will not yield to texts of Scriptures, is to jeer and flout him, for he cannot bear scorn." The intention of this book is not only to jeer at the devil and flout him but to offer ways of thinking and speaking about him (or it) that might deprive the devil of subliminal respect from Christians and give the glory to God.

CHAPTER TWO

DISBELIEVING IN
THE DEVIL

Should Christians believe in the devil? The vast majority of those who believe in the final authority of the Bible will answer in the affirmative. There may be others, whether Christians or not, who find this objectionable. Yet those who do believe in the devil can at least argue that they are being consistent. If the Bible is to be believed in its witness concerning God, why should it not be equally believable in regard to the devil? And if belief in the devil is rejected, is not belief in God sure to follow in swift order? Whatever difficulties modern people have with such a belief, all are bound to admit that the devil is taken with great seriousness in the New Testament. So much so that it is impossible to understand the New Testament correctly without seeing that the drama it records is a conflict between two kingdoms: that of God and that of the devil. The reason the Son of God appeared was to destroy the works of the devil (1 Jn 3:8). To remove this element of conflict from the Gospels would lead to a major misunderstanding of the mission of Jesus.[1]

This statement is borne out by the fact that, at every level of its witness, the New Testament takes the spiritual conflict seriously. The reality of spiritual powers of good is taken for granted in the Gospels (Mt 26:53; Lk 12:8; 15:10). Against this background the reality of opposing spiritual powers is also recognized. In the Old Testament there is considerable restraint concerning the person of Satan, who is only mentioned specifically on three occasions (Zech 3:1; Job 1—2; 1 Chron 21:1). The New Testament, however, presents us with a world under the domination of Satan.

For instance, in the Gospel of Luke, after his baptism and anointing, Jesus is tempted by the devil (4:1-13). He very quickly and significantly delivers a demon-possessed man in the synagogue at Capernaum (4:33-37). In the midst of a healing ministry he deals frequently with the demonic (4:41). He heals a woman who has been "crippled by Satan" for eighteen years (13:16), and he is finally betrayed after Satan "enters into" Judas Iscariot (22:3).

This picture of a "powerful personal agency of evil, in whom is concentrated intense opposition to the mission of Jesus"[2] is confirmed by the fourth Gospel. John speaks of Satan as the "ruler of this world" (12:31; 14:30; 16:11) who functions as the enemy of God and is a "murderer" and "the father of lies" (8:44). John also sees Satan as the power behind the betrayal of Jesus (13:27) and quotes Jesus as saying that, through his lifting up, "the prince of this world" will be driven out (12:31).

It would be possible to go on multiplying references to prove the point that in each strand of the New Testament there is a consciousness of the powers of darkness as real and malevolent entities, but it is not necessary to do so. The question is, how can we who live in a very different world from that of the New Testament, a scientific, "enlightened" and (supposedly) more sophisticated age, go on believing in the reality of such personalized powers as the devil and his demons? A number of responses are possible at this point.

UNCONDITIONAL ACCEPTANCE

It is possible to accept the picture with which the New Testament presents us quite uncritically. After all, if this is the way the New Testament teaches it, then this is the way it must be, whatever modern ways of thinking may make of it. Granted, modernity is not itself a criterion of truth. But neither are we greatly helped by unreflective repetition. This approach may show willingness to believe the Bible and to defend it, but it could miss the possibility that a modern understanding of the ways individuals and societies function may shed light back on the teaching of the New Testament.

Reading the New Testament in light of modern thought could help us to a fuller understanding of the way the power of darkness operates. We should not underestimate the power of modern thought actually to disclose further depths in the New Testament witness, and we should be concerned to read it in the light of modern knowledge, and vice versa, to see what each may reveal about the other.

UNCONDITIONAL REJECTION

A further response is to consign New Testament teaching concerning the power of evil to the dustbin of history. It belongs to a world of superstition and primitive belief out of which the human race, aided by the other more positive insights of Jesus, is emerging. In this way of thinking the only form of darkness in the world is that produced by humankind's own wrong attitudes or wrong behavior. If the New Testament symbols of the devil and the demons have any value, it is simply as an outward projection onto a cosmic screen of struggles between dark and light that are taking place within people. The real struggle is in the interior world and not in the cosmic realm, which remains morally neutral. As objective entities, the devil and demons do not exist. Rather, the devil is symbolic of corporate, structural evil produced by the social structures of human society. "Demons" are primitive ways of describing what we now know to be mental illness. Further, the old imagery of the devil is to be rejected as too simplistic, causing us to divide complicated matters into black and white.

The difficulty with maintaining this point of view is, for a Christian, twofold. First, it remains a major stumbling block that Jesus himself believed in the external existence of powers of evil. It would be impossible to argue convincingly that when Jesus entered into the world of demonic conflict he was merely pretending to believe in something he knew was not real. It might be more convincing to say that Jesus' acceptance of the devil belonged to the area of his divine accommodation to human ignorance and weakness. Becoming a human being in a particular place, at a specific time meant becoming one who shared the assumptions and beliefs of his day and culture. Were it not so it would have been impossible for Jesus to speak meaningfully in the context in which he lived. So, it could be that Jesus' apparent belief in the spiritual powers of evil is no more binding on us today than, say, the belief in a flat earth, which he probably also shared (although did not teach).

This second line of argument is worthy of some respect, if not of final agreement. It attempts to take seriously what it means for Jesus to become human in space and time. It founders on the centrality the devil has in the ministry and work of Christ. Jesus believed in the reality of the devil and was profoundly aware of a personal conflict with such a power. The temptation narratives, which must have their origin in Jesus' own self-awareness, are testimony to this. So is his saying in Luke 10:18—"I saw Satan fall like lightning from heaven"—and his climactic sense of conflict with the "prince of this world" immediately prior to his crucifixion (Jn 12:31).

The very centrality of this spiritual conflict in the mind of Jesus indicates that there is something more essential here, of more significance than any incidental accommodation (intended or otherwise) to human ignorance or to cultural conditions. The question must then be asked: in what sense can we speak of the Lordship of Christ, his ability to determine the shape of our existence, if we reject something that is so clearly part of his own way of believing? To do so begins to evacuate the confession of Jesus as Lord of any possible significance.

A second reason why rejecting the New Testament witness to the powers of darkness is problematic is because to do so involves distorting the other teachings integrally linked with it. The reason the Son of God came forth was to destroy the devil's work. If we no longer believe in the devil's work we must find another reason why the Son of God came into the world. Michael Green may have a rather bald way of saying it but he hits close to the mark when he says: "I believe the Christian doctrines of God, of man and of salvation are utterly untenable without the existence of Satan. You simply cannot write him out of the story and then imagine that the story is basically unchanged."[3]

This remark of Green's has been sharply criticized. It could be read as making belief in Satan a necessary and antecedent basis for belief in God. Possibly he does come near to giving the devil too honorable a place in the Christian scheme, but he has a point that stands. We cannot dispose of a central theme in the New Testament witness without disturbing and jeopardizing the whole—in this instance, the concept of the devil.

SYMPATHETIC BUT FAITHFUL REINTERPRETATION

Is there any mileage then in pursuing a third way, namely reinterpreting New Testament language in a way that is illuminated but not over-whelmed by modern (or should it now be postmodern) knowledge? Integral to this approach is the understanding that primitive beliefs are not necessarily wrong beliefs. It is bad practice to brand as superstition categories of thought that appear to us outmoded.

Rather than the rash assumption that contemporary thinking is necessarily superior to that of previous generations, we should recognize that in the process of rationalization, industrialization and secularization, which have so extensively shaped the Western world, we may have lost as much as we have gained. The relentless drive to reduce everything to its basic components that we may understand and control it may, in fact, mean that we fail to appreciate the wholeness of the universe. Pursuit of reason may lead to loss of intuition, pursuit of knowledge to loss of wisdom.

The modernist assumption that all knowledge can be made homogenous has led us to factor out those elements of human testimony that do not fit the mold. Yet it is precisely those things that are on the margins, things that will not fit, that are the most interesting to us. Postmodern thinking has realized that there is much to learn from "primitive" societies. The language of the devil and demons may describe elements in our existence, the consciousness of evil, that we lack language to describe in any other way. Our task is to penetrate this language, to sense what it refers to from the inside, and then to find explicatory language and vocabulary that will do justice to it in our day and age.

This approach has much to commend it, not least its sympathy and humility. The question remains, however, as to whether it is really possible to improve on the New Testament concepts of the devil and his demons or whether any attempted reinterpretation would end up missing something of crucial importance. Perhaps there is something about evil that can only be adequately expressed in any culture and at any time by using the thought forms and the language that the New Testament gives us.

Having outlined a variety of approaches, perhaps I should come clean. I characterize my own approach as that of "thoughtful acceptance" of the New Testament teaching. By this I declare my conviction that we cannot rise above or beyond what we are taught by Jesus and his apostles. Rather we find that, if we risk everything in the faith that what Jesus taught is true, we will not be disappointed. This is part of the scandal of Christian faith. I approach New Testament teaching therefore in the spirit of acceptance. But this acceptance is critical and reflective. It proceeds on the assumption that, because the New Testament teaches truth, truth will be confirmed by honest inquiry and human discovery. Modern knowledge can greatly expand our insight into the subject of evil by disclosing more fully how it is that the powers of darkness are at work in people and in societies.

In this regard it is possible to learn from those who reinterpret the

New Testament without the powers of darkness and who look instead for alternate ways of describing evil. There are certainly people who believe in such dark powers and yet misuse "devil" language to project their own inner struggles; consequently, not all that is called devil is actually devil. The New Testament, in order to understand its depth, should therefore be read in awareness of the challenges presented by these alternate interpretations. The idea that New Testament teaching is threatened by honest inquiry belongs not to the realm of faith but to the realm of unbelief.

To return to our original question: should Christians believe in the devil? Those who have followed the argument so far might expect that we should now answer this question in the affirmative. Christians ought to believe in the devil! In fact, however, I wish to assert the opposite—the devil should be the object of disbelief. Some would insist that a major problem of the church is that it doesn't believe strongly enough in the devil. My objection is the precise opposite. We believe in the devil too much. Belief in the devil does not belong in the Christian confession of faith. As Christians we confess our faith in God, maker of heaven and earth, in Jesus Christ his only Son our Lord, and in the Holy Spirit, the Lord and giver of life. We believe in God. We disbelieve in the devil.

I am playing, of course, with words, specifically the word *believe*—but not in an idle way. To believe in somebody or something implies that we believe in their existence. But it also carries overtones of an investment of faith or trust. To believe in Jesus means, or should mean, more than believing in his existence. It should involve personal trust and faith by virtue of which the power of Christ is magnified in the life of the believer. The access of Christ to an individual's life, his power of influence within him or her, is in proportion to faith. The same use of language applies in the wider world. To believe in a political leader implies more than believing in his existence; it implies faith in the system of values for which he stands and confidence in his ability to carry it through.

The reply to the question whether Christians should believe in the devil must therefore be a resounding no. When we believe in something we have a positive relationship to that in which we believe, but for the Christian a positive relationship to the devil and demons is not possible.[4] We believe in God, and on the basis of this faith, we disbelieve in the devil. It is an act of disbelief grounded in faith. This may seem to some a quibble over words, but it arises out of the very genuine and necessary concern that too many Christians have a big devil and a small God.

The editor of the I Believe . . . series of books on Christian doctrine exhibited a sound instinct and illustrates this point. Having produced a series including titles such as I Believe in Revelation, I Believe in the Historical Jesus and I Believe in the Second Coming, he could not bring himself to call the book on the devil I Believe in the Devil. Instead he changed the pattern and it was called I Believe in Satan's Downfall! Satan is not the object of Christian belief but of Christian disbelief. We believe against the devil. We resolutely refuse the devil place. Otto Weber has it right when he says:

> To be sure, as Christians we do not believe "in" the devil. The devil is not mentioned in the creed. But we do believe "against" the devil. The whole creed is simultaneously the "renunciation" of the devil. Yet the power against which faith is faith has its own reality, just as certainly as it does not have its own validity.[5]

Weber helps us to strike a balance. We do not believe in the devil but against him, and in doing so we acknowledge that the power of darkness against which we believe has its own reality. Even though it has a reality it lacks a validity—it ought not to exist because it is the contradiction of all existence. Its existence is unthinkable even as it is undeniable. It exists, but for the Christian it exists as something to be rejected and denied. The importance of this consists precisely in the fact that when Christians are to be found believing "in" the devil they succeed against their will and no doubt against their knowledge in actually increasing the devil's power.

This is seen in several of the areas to which reference was made in the first chapter. The great witch craze gathered momentum because people were too willing to believe in what the devil could do. In this mood they ascribed all manner of things to the devil. The power and presence of the devil thus became exaggerated because people were too willing to believe.

This attitude is not altogether lacking in the contemporary church. In giving greater focus to the reality of the power of darkness, renewal movements run the danger of seeing the devil where he is not, or of so exaggerating or heightening incidents or situations that the power of darkness is blown out of all proportion to its actual presence. When this happens it is scarcely distinguishable from superstition. A "demon consciousness" arises, which bears no relation to actuality, and distorts and degrades the individual. This attitude can rightly be described as neurotic religion breeding a paranoid view of reality. It produces a demonized world and renders those who hold such an attitude not a little demonic themselves.

How we *think* about evil is of great importance. C. S. Lewis's dictum about the two equal and opposite errors is right. We err both by disregarding the reality of evil and by taking it so seriously that we overestimate it or become overconscious of it so that it clouds our vision of God and his world. The resolution of this problem lies not only in our refusal to be attracted by evil but also in learning to talk about it in a way that both takes it seriously and relativizes it. Even for Christians evil can present a fair and attractive face. There is the lure of the sinister. It fascinates us and occupies our attention. The subtitle of this book—putting the power of darkness in its place—is what we should be about.

We are talking about a power that is inherently deceptive. According to Jesus the devil has been a liar from the beginning (Jn 8:44). It is in the nature of evil to deceive, and the devil has been about this task since the serpent spoke in the Garden of Eden (1 Tim 4:1; 2 Cor 11:3). One form of deception is to persuade people to disregard its existence since this anonymity opens up many opportunities. If this strategy fails then the alternative is to exaggerate its power so that excessive fear is created, which in turn allows darkness to thrive and provides a form of access for it into our lives. The Christian exists in his or her thinking within a tension of not taking the devil seriously enough on the one hand, thus coming into deception, and on the other hand, taking him too seriously and seeing him at work where he is not, thus falling into another form of deception. Right models of thought will keep our perspective clear and keep the power of darkness in its place.

Why is it that we run the risk of distortion in this area? We have already indicated that the nature of the devil is deception, falsity, untruth. When we consider the power of deception on the human life, we should realize what a great force this power of darkness has. Immense amounts of suffering are caused in the world because individuals have distorted images of God, of themselves and of other people, leading them to treat others as enemies to be feared rather than as people to be loved. The same is true on a far grander scale of the relations between nations. If people could only see one another as they are, apart from the fears, prejudices and bigotry that are produced by the powers of deception, we would be living in a different world. However, several other factors distort our perspective.

The attraction the power of darkness exerts. It is a matter of indisputable fact that people are more easily attracted by evil than by good. There is a black-hole quality that evil displays, drawing attention to itself in a way that is apparently more powerful than the good. Evil truly can display a fair face. It is the aberrations of human life that sell newspapers, inspire TV programs and become the subjects of novels. Evil has a certain inexplicable quality that eludes people and causes them to want to fathom the mystery. Perhaps people enjoy the vicarious thrill of reading or hearing of evil and tragedy.

Whatever may be the case on the secular level, an attraction is exerted by evil even over Christian minds. The popularity of books and tapes on the demonic is not purely to be attributed to the desire for greater spiritual effectiveness. There is the unhealthy and vicarious attraction of the forbidden to be reckoned with. "Demon syndrome" is a possibility even for those who should be least attracted to the demonic. It is a form of spiritual pathology. In his remarkable novel *The Name of the Rose* Umberto Eco paints just such a picture of a medieval monastery overtaken by demon-mindedness and consequently prey to all manner of delusions.[6]

Inadequacy of human language. Human language labors to describe the nature of evil adequately. This should not surprise us as language is intended to describe the positive and wholesome realities of our human existence and not the negative and chaotic powers of evil. The result is, however, that even in our language we run the danger of being too positive. Let me illustrate this by highlighting several points.

The use of *personal language* about the devil is problematic. It personalizes the devil and therefore gives him a dignity he does not deserve. To refer to the devil as "he" or "him" (as we have already done frequently) confers on the devil a form of language that, strictly speaking, refers to people who are made in the image of God. It is only as a tentative and limited analogy that it is appropriate to use personal words about the devil. Nothing in the Bible suggests the devil was made in the image of God. This is exclusively referred to human beings. Not even the angels are described as being in God's image. Its primary use is in relation to people, and it carries a sense of people who feel, love, relate and have the dignity of personhood bestowed on them by God.

We have come to see that personhood is something into which we enter by means of relationships. Exactly at this point we are imaging God since the Christian vision of God is of One who is in eternal and essential relationship. The one God exists in and as a triunity of persons. The Father is in relationship with the Son by the Spirit and cannot be the Father other than through this relationship, since without the Son he would not be the Father. So it is with the Son and with the Spirit who exists as the Other over against the Father and Son. Human beings have the divine image (a rich term) not least in their existence as people who are in embodied relationship with others. For this reason the crucial text says: "So God created humankind in his image, in the image of God he created them, male and female he created them" (Gen 1:28).

This language is problematic in reference to the devil because it would require the devil to be in relationship in such a way as to constitute a personal identity. Yet it would be more accurate to think of the devil as a nonperson, as subpersonal or antipersonal rather than personal. It would be even more accurate and satisfying if we were able to refer to the devil as "it." This same difficulty is felt by Andrew Walker, who writes:

> For myself I would rather refer to the Devil as "it" than "him," because "him" denotes someone who is a person, or at least a being who can be said to exhibit the traits of personhood. Strictly speaking, I feel that only God is truly personal and we as human beings are only persons in so far that we can be said to bear God's image. I am not sure that we can say that about the Evil One: the Devil is all that God is not.[7]

Experience suggests that many readers will stumble at this point since the idea of a "personal devil" is almost an article of faith for many. Indeed, in one church I know, belief in a personal devil is written into the church's statement of faith (very oddly in my view). On my desk as I write is a collection of reviews of a book by a leading and bestselling evangelical New Testament scholar. Several reviewers express concern (amid general approval of the book's value) over the author's opinion that to call the satan [sic] a person rather than a force "may be going too far."[8] The book is commended by some but is to be used "with caution." I return to this issue in a later chapter but for the moment would encourage readers simply to feel the difficulty, in light of the above comments, of calling the devil a "person."

A further difficulty with personal language is that it denotes *the kind of limitations that characterize personal individuality.* We are therefore led by this language to visualize the devil as an evil individual; this in turn may mean that we lose the proper sense of the pervasive nature of evil. This is not intended to suggest that the devil is omnipresent, but there is a quality about the power of darkness that is at least co-extensive with humanity. Wherever human beings are, the power of darkness lies close at hand. You may have observed that I have exhibited so far a marked preference for the phrase "power of darkness" because it might express more adequately both the pervasive and the nonhuman aspects of this reality as it is experienced by human beings.

Having said all of this about the problems of personal language it nonetheless seems impossible to speak seriously about the devil without at some point using it. I have not been able to avoid doing this myself and speaking in this way, whatever the difficulties, adds a degree of force and precision to the discussion. Jesus himself clearly used such language. Paul supplements this with the more impersonal language of "principalities and powers," suggesting the diversity of the power of darkness. But like Jesus he also consistently refers to the devil. Because Jesus thought in terms of a conflict with an adversary called the devil or Satan there must have been good reason for doing so. If we avoid this language, perhaps, we miss a vital ingredient in describing the power of darkness, namely the sense of an intelligence or an agency that is both willful and malevolent. These points will be investigated more fully at a later point.

A further difficulty of our use of language is in the area known technically as *ontology*, the study of being. Talk of the devil creates the impression that, in the order of being (God-creation-angels-humankind), there is a further order of being that also has its place—the devil and his angels. Jesus uses this language without embarrassment (Mt 25:41). But it confers legitimacy on the devil if he is thought to have an existence *of the same order* as that of God. The devil takes his place among the *dramatis personae* of the human drama and becomes a necessary, even in his own way an honored, part of human life. The devil becomes respectable and acceptable by virtue of having a place. One of the great criticisms of John Milton's epic poem *Paradise Lost* is that the devil is portrayed as a sympathetic, tragic figure in the Promethean mold. By contrast, God seems distinctly boring, "too busy being almighty to be very interesting."[9] We need to be able to assert with Otto Weber: "The power against which faith is faith has its own reality, *just as certainly as it does not have its own validity*" (italics mine).

The point is that the devil has no legitimacy. He does not have a place assigned to him by God. If he exists he exists in violation of all that is right, true and legitimate. Evil cannot be assigned an acceptable place of dignity within God's universe—it has no such place, it has no right to exist. It is total and complete aberration, even if, as such, it does not fall outside of God's providential rule. Evil exists as chaos to order, as lie to truth or darkness to light. For this reason the devil is not something or someone to be believed in: it is something or someone to be resolutely rejected and refused by those who believe in Christ. When it is argued that if we are to cease believing in a personal, ontological devil the next step would be to abandon belief in God, we are displaying a grievous error. God is the living God who possesses fullness of being and is, in Paul Tillich's terms, Being Itself. God and the devil stand in mutual contradiction. To make God's existence even notionally dependent on or akin to that of the devil is close to blasphemy.

The preferred attitude, one that accepts evil's existence but not its validity, is discerned in the words of Jesus in Luke 10:1-20. Here Jesus sends out his disciples to be his representatives in the towns and villages and to prepare the way for his coming. No doubt they go out in fear and in trepidation, wondering what awaits them. In the event, they are overjoyed at what they experience. The most exciting thing is that "even the demons submit to us in your name" (v. 17). Jesus quickly tells them how he has been aware of their effectiveness in this realm. "I saw Satan fall like lightning from heaven" (v. 18). He goes on to speak of the authority he has given to them: "I have given you authority to trample on snakes and scorpions and to overcome all the power of the enemy; nothing will harm you" (v. 19). But then, significantly, he directs their attention away from the demons and back to God: "However do not rejoice that the demons submit to you, but rejoice that your names are written in heaven" (v. 20).

It is almost as if Jesus is warning his disciples about the dangers of being overconcerned with or overfocused on the demons. The source of rejoicing is not the negative fact that we have power over demons but the positive one that our names are written in heaven and that we have a secure relationship and destiny in God. Not even victory over the demons is a valid source of spiritual emotion and sustenance. Encounter with the demonic either in thought or in action can quickly lead to a loss of perspective due to its mesmeric and deceptive power. It can be a heady experience, leading people engaged in deliverance ministry, for instance, to take pride in their own spiritual authority, in the fact that demons do what they are told. There are deceptive illusions of spiritual power here, at the root of why some such people go wrong. The only way to maintain perspective is to fill our horizons and hearts with the knowledge of God. Only then can we see the power of darkness for the beggarly and empty thing that it is.

Christians should exercise disbelief in the devil by actively refusing to give it the credibility it keenly desires but does not deserve. The next two chapters are concerned with how we may do this more adequately.

CHAPTER THREE

ANALYZING EVIL I
Its Essence

The more the devil is trivialized the easier it becomes to dismiss him. Therefore we should avoid trivializing evil. When we speak about the devil we immediately conjure up a host of images that have been passed on to us by our culture. Satan is presented as a horned satyr-like creature with a long, pointed, leering, ugly face and a three-pronged fork. Such images are drawn from pagan mythology rather than the Bible. The effect of them is to make of the devil a character that bears no relation to life as most of us know it and that may be casually dismissed as a piece of superstitious nonsense. This represents a victory for the opposition. To be able to take evil seriously we need more sophisticated ways of understanding it.

The Bible does not offer us crude images of the devil but speaks in terms of the invisible power that the devil uses. It is true that the devil is pictured as a serpent (Gen 3:1; Rev 20:2), but it is more usual for the *activity* of the devil to come into view. Satan is a liar and a murderer (Jn 8:44; Acts 5:3), a betrayer (Lk 22:3), a destroyer (1 Pet 5:8), an accuser and a slanderer (Rev 12:10). He keeps people bound and in prison (Lk 13:16) and tempts them to evil (1 Cor 7:5). He is an enemy of God and of righteousness (Mt 13:39; Acts 13:10). It is, therefore, the influence and effect of evil in the world that receive attention rather than pictorial descriptions. This is a clue to how we may envisage or describe the essence of evil in the world. Properly considered, what the Bible teaches us is not a trivial, lurid piece of superstition but a sophisticated and profound description of what human beings experience in life.

This chapter more fully penetrates into the nature of evil by engaging in dialogue with four recent thinkers who have reflected extensively on the topic. None of them is regarded as offering an entirely satisfactory analysis of the essence of evil, but each of them has something to contribute to our understanding. These insights will be utilized in an attempt to describe the essence of evil insofar as we can. In the next chapter our analysis of evil will continue with an investigation of its form.

EVIL AS DISCREATIVITY

We begin with a short examination of the theologian Edwin P. Lewis, who took particular interest in the concept of the demonic.[1] Lewis began his theological pilgrimage as a liberal and moved from there to being an evangelical before taking up a Zoroastrian position. In Zoroastrianism's concept of an eternal dualism—a conflict between Angra Mainyu, the principle of the lie, and Ahura Mazda, the principle of truth—some background to biblical thought is found.

Lewis came to conceive of a world composed of three eternal existents—God (who is creative), the Adversary (who is discreative) and the Residue (which is uncreative).[2] This explains the phenomena of existence. God is creatively at work in the world, giving it shape and purpose. His creativity is opposed by the Adversary, which continually discreates and disrupts God's creative work. The world itself is the Residue, not itself creative, but being acted on by the two opposing forces of good and evil. Thus humankind lives in a world caught between these two forces and is free to work with that which makes for creativity or discreativity. By good thoughts, good words and good deeds it can work with the creative to overcome the discreative.

There are echoes here of the concept of the Force, popularized in the

Star Wars trilogy. The Force is essentially one but is composed of a good side and a disruptive side. The dark side takes form in individuals who yield to its attractions. It is possible to use the Force for good or ill, and human, as well as other life forms', choices count in this process. Those who work with the good side of the Force achieve a degree of spiritual enlightenment just as those who identify with the dark side achieve a form of malevolent spirituality and power.

What can be said about Lewis (or about the Force!)? There is an understanding of reality here that has its own attraction. The creative-discreative-uncreative concept takes account of the actual phenomena at work in the world. There are forces of good and forces that oppose the good and seek to undo it wherever it is found. This is true to the sense of struggle characteristic of all life. If the good is to be maintained it can only be at the cost of continual output of creative energy. Where this ceases, the forces of decay and discreativity are at work. In this sense, it is easier to be discreative since nothing positive needs to be achieved—it is simply a matter of undoing what the good has done. This explains the attraction that evil has for people—it takes nothing to side with the forces of darkness but much to expend the energy that makes for good. The discreative is a dynamic of unraveling and undoing which requires only the ability to let oneself be carried along. Sloth is of the essence of sin. This also explains how human beings can be "good" or "evil" and puts a value on moral decision and on the direction of our lives.

These elements in Lewis's thought are attractive. However, from the perspective of Christian theology his overall scheme must be rejected because it tends to make evil coeternal with good and thereby denies the sovereignty and supremacy of a good God. If the Adversary is coeternal with God, then God is not the God of the Christian revelation, from whom all things come, in whom they exist and to whom they are finally directed. Despite this, the concept of discreativity adds to our understanding of how evil is at work in the world, seeking to discreate what

God has created. The Adversary opposes the work of God to thwart it. Human beings are caught in this conflict but are able by the direction and commitment of their lives to invest in the creative or the discreative side. These are useful concepts, and they potentially enhance our understanding of the nature of evil.

EVIL AS NOTHINGNESS

Karl Barth was the outstanding theologian of the early twentieth century with definite opinions on most things. For the most part Barth's theology is a startling restatement of orthodox Christianity as understood in the Reformed tradition. In the transition from a liberal to an evangelical theology, Barth was strongly influenced by Johann Christoph Blumhardt and his son Christoph Friedrich (who will be discussed later). Both were acquainted with encounters with the demonic. In addition, Barth lived in Germany at the time of Hitler's rise to power and immediately recognized the anti-Christian nature of National Socialism, unlike the majority of his fellow Christians. He was inclined to take seriously the power of evil in a way many other theologians did not and in doing so developed a quite distinct concept of evil as "Nothingness" (*das Nichtige*).

The concept of "Nothingness"[3] should be understood within Barth's theology as a whole. It is characteristic that he attempts to escape static categories of thought and to conceive of God and his work dynamically. Nothingness is Barth's conception of a power in opposition to God that has a negatively dynamic character. He freely admits the term is one he has fashioned himself and should be taken with a grain of salt. But, in his belief, it does express briefly, tersely and strongly insights that are truly biblical.[4] His intention is not to suggest that evil does not exist but that it exists in negativity, without any right to exist, without any value or positive strength.

The translators of *Church Dogmatics* debated also whether to render *das Nichtige* as the *nihil*, the "null," "the negative" or the "non-existent."[5]

Its existence is paradoxical, and its nature is perversion.[6] The fact of Nothingness (that is to say of evil) is revealed through Christ in the sense that its hostility to God is revealed in its hostility to Christ.[7] At the same time Nothingness is under God's control, and Christ's incarnation is God's answer to it. Nothingness takes form as real death, real devil, real hell and the real sin of human beings.[8]

> In Him, i.e., in contradistinction to Him, Nothingness is exposed in its entirety as the adversary which can destroy both body and soul in hell, as the evil one which is also the destructive factor of evil and death that stands in sinister conflict against the creature and its creator, not merely as an idea which man may conceive and to which he can give allegiance but as the power which invades and subjugates and carries him away captive, so that he is wholly and utterly lost in the face of it.[9]

Barth insists that our knowledge of this evil reality is not a matter of speculation but a clear deduction from the self-disclosure of God in Jesus Christ.

> It is not a speculation but a description which even the veriest child can understand simply to say of evil in the first instance that it is what God does not will. But to say this is also to say that it is something which He never did nor could will, nor ever will nor can. It is thus that evil is characterised, judged and condemned in the self-disclosure of the living person of Jesus Christ. As opposition to God, it is that which is simply opposed to His will, and from eternity, in time and to all eternity negated, rejected, condemned and excluded by his will.[10]

The term "Nothingness" can be seen to have value in that it attempts to describe the essence of evil. Evil is that about which nothing positive can be said or thought. It exists in negation and is itself wholly negative. This poses the question: how can such a power exist in a world that God has made? Where is its origin? The traditional doctrine has been that evil has its origin in the free will of humans and angels. It is the freedom of both to go astray that is the point at which evil originates in a good universe. However Barth resists such an idea. The concept of a pre-mundane angelic fall is rejected scathingly as "one of the bad dreams of the older dogmatics."[11] He rejects the idea because, in his reckoning, angels do not and cannot fall. The devil was never an angel but a liar and a murderer from the beginning.[12] Verses in the Bible that point in the direction of an angelic fall are too uncertain and obscure to build on.[13] Nothingness is an alien factor that can be attributed neither to the positive will and work of God nor to the activity of the creature.[14] Yet neither can it exist independently of the will of God since this would be to deny his Lordship.[15]

We are confronted with a genuine difficulty in understanding. Nothingness is real. It is not nothing and yet it has nothing in common with God or his creatures. It must therefore exist in a third way peculiar to itself. In this sense only, Nothingness *is*.[16] Here Barth is keen to stress the invalid nature of evil. It has no right to exist as if it were a creature of God or on the same terms. Its existence is not a planned and willed existence as is that of humankind. We are faced with something that is real but has no right to be.

Barth further rejects the idea of an angelic fall because he resents the equation of angels and demons. He sees the association of the two in much theology as "primitive and fatal."[17] He takes great delight in the subject of angels and deals with them in a novel and creative way, with the intention of restoring their "permanent residence visas" in Christian theology.[18] Angels are beings that are summoned into existence wherever God is at work among human beings. They are witnesses of God who precede, accompany, surround and follow the coming kingdom of God.[19] Angels "slip between our fingers" because they are free from any personal desire for power or lordship. They belong fully to God and in no sense to themselves.[20] Because of this, and unlike human beings, angels cannot deviate. Therefore they cannot become fallen creatures.

In this context Barth turns his attention to the demons, the opponents of the ambassadors of God. He finds this subject distasteful and is only willing to cast "a momentary glance" at the demons. Because demons thrive on attention—and to contemplate them too intensely raises the danger that we too may become a little demonic—a quick, sharp glance is all that is necessary and legitimate.[21] The demons exist in a "dreadful fifth or sixth dimension of existence" and are constantly active "like the tentacles of an octopus."[22] They exist as an army never in repose and always on the march invading and attacking with falsehood as their manner of being.[23] God and the devil or angels and demons should not even be spoken of in the same breath. Angels and demons are related asymmetrically, as creation and chaos, life and death, light and darkness. They are not two subdivisions of the same genus.[24]

According to Barth, we cannot look for the origin of evil in a supposed fall of angels. Where then is such an origin to be found? Here he is at his most novel. Nothingness, he argues, has its origin in the "No" of God, which is implied by his original creative "Yes." In other words, in saying yes to the creation and calling it into being, God uttered an implied no, a rejection of that which is evil. And this no, being also a powerful word of God, has created the realm of Nothingness. Nothingness is that which God rejects, opposes, negates and dismisses in the act of creation.[25]

> Nothingness is that which God does not will. It lives only by the fact that it is that which God does not will. But it does live by this fact, for not only what God wills, but what he does not will, is potent and must have a real correspondence. What really corresponds to that which God does not will is Nothingness.[26]

Exegetically, Barth roots his case in the chaos of Genesis 1:2. When it is affirmed here that "the earth was a formless void and darkness covered the face of the waters," this is the chaos of Nothingness that God despised in his creative work, the lower sphere that God passed by without a halt. It is the sphere of chaos that behind God's back has assumed the self-contradictory character of reality.[27]

What are we to make of these remarkable mental gymnastics? In support of Barth we recognize his originality in formulating a new theory of the origin of evil. He seeks to understand how evil can exist in a way contrary to the will of God but nevertheless in the sphere of the will of God. He maintains fully the objective reality of evil and of the devil and demons, although he rejects the concept of a fall of angels as giving too much dignity to the devil. But perhaps his greatest strength is the evident contempt for evil and the demonic he demonstrates. The word *Nothingness* is novel, but it expresses the nature of evil as a negative force and the fact that it exists improperly in a way that is not planned or purposed by God. It is abhorred and abhorrent.

The crucial conclusion to be drawn from this is that evil exists parasitically. It draws its energy from that which exists authentically in God's will by sucking out the life of what God has created. It draws its existence from the living creation on which it trades. The significance of this understanding of evil will be investigated in other contexts.

The concept of evil as a parasite is deeply rooted in Christian thought. Augustine saw evil as *privatio boni*, an absence of goodness rather than a creature in its own right. This conforms to the concept of discreativity that we have already noted. Evil cannot create; it can only feed on or destroy what is created.

Here again is a reason why Christians should practice disbelieving in the devil. The demons and the devil welcome it when they get undue attention from Christians. They are boosted. It is a form of energy from which they exist. Barth's concept of Nothingness, therefore, has much to commend it in describing the essence of evil.

We cannot, however, follow Barth in his attempt to explain how evil has come to be. He must be criticized for his exegesis of Scripture. His use of the chaos in Genesis 1:2 as proof of his theory is a classic *eisegesis* whereby he discovers his own theory of evil in the biblical account of creation.[28] Barth is presenting rich ideas, but they are hard to square with the text. On the face of it Genesis 1:1-2 is a bald suggestion that God made the world in two stages: bringing the chaos into being and then establishing order within it. It is not an explanation of evil.[29] His concept of the origin of Nothingness has more the character of a speculation than an exposition of firm biblical truth.[30] In fairness to him, the exegetical basis of an angelic fall is also problematic, as we shall see.

Barth's concept must also be faulted for its theological inadequacy. If God gives rise to Nothingness by virtue of the "No!" implied by his creative "Yes!" we must ask the question, was it God's will that his no should have this effect, or was God powerless to prevent it happening? In either case we are left with a problem. Either God wills evil and gives rise to it (in which case his goodness is compromised) or he does not will it yet is powerless to prevent it happening (in which case his sovereignty is compromised). To argue, as Barth does, that it is God's nonwilling that gives rise to Nothingness has been described as a "curiously far-fetched and concocted notion."[31] Barth's concept renders sin and evil not so much absurd as inevitable.

Barth's concept does not stand up to scrutiny. At the same time he has given the analysis of evil some unusually valuable attention and the concept of Nothingness is well suited to a description of the essence of evil. The realism and yet contempt with which he casts his short, sharp glance at the demonic kingdom should be taken as a model for those who reflect on this subject, not least for its treatment in this book. There are excellent theological and spiritual instincts at work here. In the next chapter an alternative understanding of the origin of evil will be attempted. But, as with the concept of discreativity, Barth's concept of Nothingness will be pressed into service in the attempt to state a more adequate analysis of the nature of evil.

EVIL AND "INTERIORITY"

A wide-ranging and highly perceptive study of this whole area has been attempted by New Testament scholar Walter Wink, which no further work in this area will be able to ignore.[32] Wink's work deserves a great deal of attention because of the insights that it offers into the nature of evil. He takes the biblical witness concerning the devil, demons, principalities and powers with the utmost seriousness and finds the language of spiritual power pervading the New Testament.

> On every page of the New Testament one finds the terminology of power: those incumbents, offices, structures, roles, institutions, ideologies, rituals, agents and spiritual influences by which power is established and exercised.[33]

To do justice to this dimension of human experience we need to have an appropriate terminology. In the Bible this is found by the use of such terms as the devil, demons and many others. Far from being "primitive" such language is actually highly sophisticated in describing life as it is. When confronted with certain experiences we find it difficult to avoid such words as *satanic* or *demonic* in order to describe them adequately. These concepts cannot be reduced to merely psychological or sociological entities, since to do this is to miss completely the spiritual dimension of reality.[34]

Yet the mythological language of the Bible needs to be reinterpreted. As far as Wink is concerned the "Powers" do not have a separate spiritual existence from the earthly reality through which they manifest themselves. The spiritual powers are to be understood as the "innermost essence" of earthly realities. To illustrate:

> a "mob spirit" does not hover in the sky waiting to leap down on an unruly crowd at a football match. It is the actual spirit consellated when the crowd reaches a certain critical flashpoint of excitement and frustration. It comes into existence in that moment, causes people to act in ways of

which they would not have dreamed themselves capable, and then ceases to exist at the moment the crowd disperses.[35]

This innermost essence Wink proposes to call *interiority*. It is necessary to explain the realities of human existence. His thesis is that "the New Testament's 'principalities and powers' is a generic category referring to the determining forces of physical, psychic and social existence. These powers usually consist of an outer manifestation and an inner spirituality or interiority."[36] In developing his thinking, Wink then goes on to apply his concept of interiority to the specific features of the New Testament witness. Satan, for instance, "did not begin life as an idea, but in experience."[37] The context for Satan is that of an actual encounter with something or someone that leads to the positing of his existence. What is this encounter?

Wink points here to an ambiguity in the Bible's witness. In the Old Testament Satan especially is described as a servant of God and has the role of an *agent provocateur* or of a public prosecutor. He functions as an adversary, as "that actual inner or collective voice of condemnation that any sensitive person hears tirelessly repeating accusations of guilt or inferiority."[38] In sections of the New Testament Satan is portrayed as "God's holy sifter" and sometimes as God's "enforcer," called in to work us over when more gentle methods will not succeed.

> When God cannot reach us through our conscious commitment, sometimes there is no other way to get our attention than to use the momentum of our consciousness to slam us up against the wall. Heavenly jujitsu, practiced by God's "enforcer," this meat-fisted, soul-sifting Satan—servant of the living God![39]

In all of these roles Satan is actually useful and, according to Wink, is not evil personified. Rather, Satan is the one who offers us choices, thereby testing us and helping us to develop conscious obedience to God by refusing the possibilities to which he points. Wink's view of Satan is that "the conscious devil is useful; the unconscious devil is perilous."[40] He means by this that if we are aware what is happening, then we are consciously able to refuse the temptation. If we are not aware we are in trouble.

Because the devil is useful in this regard he argues that Satan has been persistently maligned. The devil is not all bad. It needs to be noted that, although he uses the language of "Satan" and "the devil," Wink has actually demythologized the biblical concepts and reinterpreted them in terms of interiority, while attempting to remain true to the sense of encounter with evil. In other words, the devil as an independent entity does not exist but has been absorbed into the interiority of human experiences.

How then does Satan, the servant of God, become the evil one, the enemy of God, the father of lies, the archfiend of Christian theology? *Agents provocateurs* have a tendency to overstep their mandate and Satan appears to have "evolved from a trustworthy intelligence-gatherer into a virtually autonomous and invisible suzerain within a world ruled by God."[41] Wink opens up for us here the intriguing possibility that Satan may originally have been created by God to exercise his "sifting" role within creation but has gone too far in the exercise of his provocative role. The "fall of Satan" could then be regarded as an attempt to push the boat out too far. Wink, however, cannot mean this literally because Satan has no independent existence. Satan's fall, for him, did not take place in time or in the universe in any external sense but in the human psyche.[42]

By human rejection of God, Satan has become "the symbolic repository of the entire complex of evil existing in the present order."[43] Because Wink defines the powers as interiority he must seek for a shift toward evil in this realm—not in some fall of angels but in the interior life of humanity, that is in human sin. Satan is the expression of the corporate interiority of such a fallen race.

> Satan is the real interiority of a society that idolatrously pursues its own enhancement as the highest good. Satan is the spirituality of an epoch, the

peculiar constellation of alienation, greed, inhumanity, oppression and entropy that characterises a specific period of history as a consequence of human decisions to tolerate and even further such a state of affairs.[44]

There is no doubt that, for those who wish to investigate this realm in the future, Wink's books will be essential reading. As with the other thinkers who have been reviewed in this chapter there will be a point at which disagreement becomes necessary, but there is much to learn from Wink's approach. Several areas in particular are worth further comment.

1. All the time he is seeking to work out his understanding in the light of the Bible's teaching and, in particular, to do justice to the role Satan plays as a servant of God, particularly in the Old Testament, which has a marked tendency to ascribe evil directly to God (e.g., Ex 4:24-26; 1 Sam 16:14-16). The New Testament is far more "dualist" in the sense of recognizing the activity of an evil power in the world, which, although not inspired by God, is nevertheless under God's control. Wink's account of Satan as an *agent provocateur* who oversteps the mark is thus an intriguing insight—although not the only way of interpreting the data.

2. Wink offers a highly sophisticated analysis of evil that is credible in terms of both human experience and the New Testament's concern with the power that opposes God. In particular he illuminates the way in which evil is actually operative—moving away from an over-personalized portrayal of evil, whereby evil spirits "hover in the air" effectively disconnected from the structures within which human beings live and operate.

Instead evil manifests itself in the realities of human life and society. More than this, he indicates that evil actually draws its negative strength and energy by preying on the energy of sin, which is to be found in humankind and human society. This is a highly significant insight. The devil is only as strong as human beings allow him to be. In referring to

James 4:7—"Submit yourselves therefore to God. Resist the devil and he will flee from you"—he makes the point that, far from being omnipotent, the devil knows his place and can be resisted.[45] The power of darkness grows in strength and energy as human beings invest their lives, their time and their attention in it.

Thus, as the human race expands in size and involvement in personal and corporate sin, so the power of darkness grows. Conversely, when humans shun sin, the power of darkness is weakened. Its only power is the power of deception and its ability to draw its own energy from disordered, disorientated and degraded humanity. The power of darkness cannot therefore be overcome by purely "spiritual" means. Binding the devil, rebuking the devil and engaging in spiritual warfare will not avail if we do not deal with the supply lines of sin that enable the power of darkness to replenish itself parasitically from the human race.

Unlike Wink, we do not consider that the devil can be denied some form of objective existence. But we do follow his train of thought in saying that the vitality of the devil is parasitic and his strength substantially drawn from humanity. It depends on the credibility and attention that is given to him as well as on the ignorance that enables him to do his work. The power that the devil has is dependent on that which humankind gives him. Essentially its power is that of deception. The effect of this must inevitably be that, in the fight, we must pay more attention to depriving Satan of sustenance by working for the personal and social salvation of humanity. Correspondingly we need to expose and confound the lies with which the darkness enthralls and captivates humans.

We must further disagree with Wink in the overpositive picture he paints of Satan. Wink is falling victim to the fair face of evil. Satan is, in his view, valuable as a servant of God and is worthy of respect in that role. Satan begins to be assimilated to God himself. Wink quotes with approval the following story of a dialogue between Sidney Harris and his daughter.

My little nine-year-old girl said to me, "Daddy, there's something peculiar about the whole story of God and the devil and hell. It just doesn't hold together." "Oh" I said, "and why doesn't it hold together?" "Well" she continued, "God is supposed to love good people and the devil is supposed to favor bad people. Right? The good people go to God, but the bad people go to hell, where the devil punishes them forever. Isn't that the story?" When I agreed that it was, she continued, "It doesn't make sense. In that case the devil couldn't be the enemy of God. I mean, if the devil really was on the side of the bad people, he wouldn't punish them in hell, would he? He'd treat them nicely and be kind to them for coming over to his side. He'd give them candy and presents and not burn them up." "You've got a point," I said. "So how do you work it out?" She thought for a moment and then she asserted, "It seems to me that if the whole story is true, then the devil is secretly on the side of God, and is just pretending to be wicked. He works for God as a kind of secret agent, testing people to find out who's good or bad, but not really fighting against God." "That's remarkable," I exclaimed. "Do you think there's any proof?" "Well," she concluded, "here's another thing. If God is really all-powerful, no devil would have a chance against him. So, if a devil really exists, it must be because he's secretly in cahoots with God!"[46]

These words of wisdom from a nine-year-old child confirm Wink in his opinion. According to this train of thought evil ceases to be evil and begins to become partly good. With this we are in danger of losing a sense of abhorrence at evil by treating it as an orderly part of God's plan. Satan does not have a legitimate place and role in human experience. However, his illegitimate and invalid activity is even so taken up by God and, through God's creative sovereignty alone, made to serve the purposes of God. Satan is not and never will be a friend of humanity, but there is a God who is able to make the activity of Satan serve an ultimately good, though distant, purpose.

Evil as Godforsaken Space

A further conversation partner in this discussion concerning the nature and origin of evil is the German Reformed theologian Jürgen Moltmann, who draws on Jewish traditions to explore the idea of *creatio ex nihilo*, or "creation out of nothing." We saw in examining Karl Barth how the idea of creation from that which was "a formless void" (Gen 1:2) has played a significant role in understanding evil. Christian theologians developed the idea that when God created he did not create out of preexistent matter, since this would suggest the existence of something alongside God. Nor did he create out of himself, since this would suggest that the world was in some sense divine. Instead he created out of nothing. For some this raised further questions (some might think them meaningless) about the exact nature of this "nothing" (or *nihil*). This is the arena into which Moltmann steps.

Building on the Jewish thinker Isaac Luria's concept of the *zimzum*—which means "concentration" and "contraction"—Moltmann advances the idea that, since God is omnipotent and fills all things, he must first create a *nihil* (think of it as an empty space) within which to create a world outside of himself.[47] To create the space God must withdraw his presence and restrict his power (hence "contraction") in an act of self-humbling and self-limitation. Creation can then be "let be" within this space as something other than God but still embraced by God.

However, for God to withdraw from anywhere leaves that space a literally Godforsaken space and calls forth a Nothingness, which is identified with hell and absolute death—the negation of God.[48] It is demonic. As creation is "let be" within this space, it exists under a constant threat of nonbeing, but the Nothingness that threatens it also threatens God and, as such, is a demonic power. By means of self-isolation from the divine being, otherwise known as sin and godlessness, creatures come under the threat of this *nihil*.[49]

Moltmann packs around this image a series of further reflections. Creation is also an act of salvation since God preserves creation from the threat of the *nihil*. The humility and self-limitation of God displayed in the act of creation is continued when Christ enters creation, taking human destiny on himself and enduring, on the cross, the demonic onslaught of the *nihil* in such a way as to overcome it.[50] Finally, as the outcome of this involvement with humankind in its suffering, God's purpose is to "de-restrict" himself and so to transfigure creation in God's glorifying "boundlessness."[51]

It is as well to remember that Moltmann's theology has been described as "Christian poetics" that oscillate between poetry and exegesis without sufficient rigor.[52] It is hard to see how biblical exegesis gives rise to this theory. Its novelty suggests that it has not previously been discovered in the text with any consistency. It might well be argued that he is engaging in his own form of myth-making and is concocting, or adapting, a creation myth, which introduces an alternative way of thinking about the origin of the world and of the evil that threatens it.

It seems to me that Moltmann is "playing" with ideas—but this is a legitimate thing to do. What his particular version has to commend it is an account of how God's creative work gives rise *of necessity* to the threat to creation we associate with the demonic. God does not create evil as such, but it is a necessary consequence of his creative activity. This illuminates evil's origin yet does not directly implicate God in it. This is a similar structure of thought to what we will later examine as the "free will defense": God creates a free world and a *necessary* consequence of its freedom—and therefore of God's creation—is the possibility of sin and evil within it.

Although we have found important points of disagreement with each of the thinkers with whom we have dialogued, we have also found that each of them offers important insights that could contribute toward the understanding of the nature of evil. Many standard ideas that Christians have of the power of darkness serve only to trivialize it and thus make it easy to reject.

We need to construct an understanding that is so authentic in what it describes that it must be taken seriously. The concept of a discreative adversary helps toward this. The concept of Nothingness further helps to comprehend the negative manner of existence of this discreative power. The concept of interiority helps us to see how this power is at work—not "up in the air" in the sense of being separate from the matrix of life, but in the earthly realities with which we are familiar, where the battle rages and of which there is a spiritual, invisible dimension. In this way it gathers its energy and strength. It is with the reality of evil in this sphere that we are called to wrestle. We do not wrestle against flesh and blood, but it is over flesh and blood that the invisible battle is fought. It is flesh and blood that makes itself available to the invisible powers that afflict their existence. The notion of the *zimzum* offers us a way of understanding how God's creative purpose and action has necessary outcomes that are a threat to creation.

Having attempted to express something of the essence and nature of evil, we will now attempt to analyze its form. In the course of this we hope to utilize some of the insights gained up to this point.

CHAPTER FOUR

ANALYZING EVIL II
Its Form

In analyzing the essence of evil in the previous chapter we found help from thinkers of the present and recent past. It was also necessary to question some of their perspectives. Now the task is to develop a coherent overall picture. This will involve asking what may be an unanswerable question: where did evil come from? By way of an answer, Robert Cook has suggested that there can only be four possibilities within the framework of Christian theology: "Logically its source must either be a created entity beyond our universe as traditional theology assumes, or in God himself, or in the structures of our created universe, or in the human race."[1] This is a useful starting point, and the options are worth reviewing in a preliminary way.

- As we have noted and will further develop—in order to question it—traditional opinion in the church's history has favored the idea of an angelic fall or catastrophe, the misuse of angelic freedom to precipitate a rebellion against God and so to initiate the drama of evil. This remains an opinion but has never formally been given the status of a dogma, an irreversible teaching, of the church. While to be treated with respect, other ways of understanding the issue are possible.

- To locate the origin of evil in some kind of "dark side" in God opens up fatal difficulties and assimilates evil into the divine existence. It is true that there is progression in the Bible in the revelation, or the apprehension, of God. Christians would struggle to attribute certain actions to God as they know him in Christ (such as the command to commit genocide) as some Old Testament texts do. But neither are they comfortable with the idea that throughout the biblical story God is "working out his dark side" and maturing. We share Cook's opinion that "neither a formerly evil God nor a formerly ignorant or immature one is worthy of Christian theology."[2]

- Attributing the origin of evil to the structure of creation as a kind of residual "black noise" left over from creation out of the primordial chaos is Cook's preferred option (but only if pressed!).[3] We noted in chapter one how Walter Brueggemann tends in this direction, and we saw in the last chapter how Barth's idea of Nothingness and Moltmann's of Godforsaken space locate evil structurally as the reverse and necessary side of the good creation. We expressed concern about the exegetical support for these positions, but against this it might be said that there is a limited exegetical basis for the traditional opinion.

- The fourth option locates the origin of evil on the level of humankind itself and in the human displacement of God, which is called sin. If the Bible leaves the origins of sin in a pre-creation fall of angels unexplored, the same cannot be said for human fallenness. This theme lies at the heart of the biblical story and in itself this suggests this fourth option is worth reconsidering.

Tom Noble builds on Cook's framework. If we exclude the second option listed above, that God himself is the origin of evil, Noble believes that each of the three remaining options offers important insights into evil, which can be substantiated to an extent from within the Scriptures and the theological tradition.[4] We will return to his proposals at the end of the chapter. As we work toward a coherent statement, we first set out ten steps, each of which analyzes more fully the form of evil and the issues surrounding it.

STEP ONE

Evil is known in its most obvious and concrete form in the sinful behavior of human beings, the inhumanity of humans. The Christian analysis of humankind is that we are fallen. There is an immense gulf between what we ought to be and what we are, between our *ontology* (what we have the potential to be) and our *existence* (what we succeed in being). Genesis 3 describes in narrative form the truth about the first man and woman, about humankind generally and about each person in particular. Adam did first what all of us do. We rebel against God and fail to rise in obedient response to his love and grace. When the Bible deals with the subject of sin and human evil it offers two pivotal points: that to do with Adam, which is concerned with sin's nature and origin, and that to do with Christ, which deals with overcoming sin and its resolution.

Yet the narrative suggests that human beings fall prey to temptation, so there is that which precedes their fall and tempts them toward it. This is indicated in Genesis 3 by the serpent's presence in the Garden, when the possibility is posed of rejecting God's command. The snake could of course be a symbol of the lower nature to which human beings give way and in Jewish interpretation is usually taken this way. But the New Testament interprets it in terms of an external tempting power called "that ancient serpent, who is the devil, or Satan" (Rev 20:2). In understanding evil we need to see that it takes form in human sin but that this itself is preceded by temptation. Emil Brunner puts it like this:

> What is evident is this: that in this classic description of the Fall, there is already a force of temptation outside man which suggests evil to man. This means that man did not himself invent evil. Man is too small, too weak, too closely connected with his senses to be the inventor of evil.[5]

This leads us to the second step in the analysis.

STEP TWO

Humankind is affected by powers greater than itself and is their victim. These greater powers are described in the Bible in a variety of ways. For instance, the apostle Paul speaks of sin as if it were a superhuman influence (Rom 6:12-23), he refers to the seductive power of the law in a similar way (Rom 7:5-11), and he speaks of the cosmic realm of "principalities and powers" (Eph 6:12) with which humanity is in conflict.

The nature of the "powers" beyond and greater than people is much debated in recent theology, no doubt because they provide a way of discussing from Scripture the influence of sociological and cultural structures. The suggestion has already been noted that, whereas the demons of the Gospels are the supposed causes of afflictions now treated by physicians and psychiatrists, the principalities and powers correspond to the concerns of politicians and sociologists, namely the corporate structures of human society.[6]

The debate concerning the powers embraces a spectrum of opinion, which is inclined at one end to identify them as angelic powers and human social structures but nothing sinister,[7] and at the other end to see them as distinct supernatural agencies of a personal and sinister kind.[8] Those who stand in the middle find an absence of distinction between earthly and spiritual realities in the belief that such dualism is foreign to the holistic assumptions of the biblical writers. The references in the New Testament to powers, thrones, authorities, elemental spirits and the like are deemed to be thoroughly ambiguous, encompassing both human structures and a transcendent dimension involving spiritual powers of good and evil kinds.[9]

The subject of the powers will be discussed more thoroughly in a later chapter. Our concern at this point is simply to demonstrate the reality of suprapersonal forces to which humanity is vulnerable and which include the religious, intellectual, moral and political forces under whose influence humanity exists. Hendrik Berkhof asserts that in addition to the interpersonal, human dimensions of sin:

> We must distinguish a suprapersonal aspect which is based not so much on the mentality of persons as on the driving force inherent both in the institutions of our established society and in the anonymous powers of current modes of behaviour, taboos, traditions or the dictates of fashion. Of course both aspects hang together. First personal sin broadens itself assuming an interpersonal shape and then, continuing, it concentrates or institutionalises itself in suprapersonal magnitudes. It is the experience of those who manage to wrest themselves free from being blinded by interpersonal forces to take up the challenge of love, that individual good will seem to accomplish little or nothing against all those forces which inexorably dictate to individuals a certain pattern of conduct—the business, the interest of the party, the needs of society, custom, fashion, public opinion, the ideology (Western or Eastern) etc. One who tries to do something against it is usually thrown aside or gets crushed under the wheels. Very few possess the strength and the courage to take this risk.[10]

Human beings are born into an ongoing story in which they are preceded by other human beings who are fallen and sinful. They are vulnerable to suprahuman powers. This still does not answer the question of the tempting power that preceded the first humans in particular and the whole human race in general.

So we proceed to the third step.

STEP THREE

Further clarification is required as to how powers that are created by God and are part of his good creation (Col 1:16) can become distorted and evil. Here we make reference to the "demonic." It is widely recognized by Christian theologians that there is an irrational, surd-like power at work in human society, which threatens and distorts existence, an alien power of deceit "out of which have poured into human existence incredible forces of disintegration and destruction."[11] These forces create "a sense of helplessness in the face of some movements or situations for which no-one seems directly responsible and which no-one seems able to control."[12] The demonic has therefore reemerged as a valid concept in much modern theology. In a work first published in 1963, Paul Tillich wrote:

> The symbol of the demonic does not need justification as it did thirty years ago, when it was reintroduced into theological language. It has become a much-used and much-abused term to designate antidivine forces in individual and social life.[13]

Different theologians mean different things by the term. For some it means the exaltation of aspects of created reality to the level of ultimate importance and absolutist control, for others a more specifically spiritual reality. It is a recognition in accordance with the Bible that evil is not adequately described unless we factor in an irrational and malevolent force at work in the world, which can cause things to go wrong.

STEP FOUR

To make sense of the demonic requires a further step. It is congenial to the modern mind to speak of the demonic in impersonal terms, since it enables us to recognize the existence of irrational evil while avoiding the problematic and pictorial language associated with "the devil." Yet, as noted, in the ministry of Jesus and at his cross the suprahuman power of darkness which enslaves humanity and which is the very presupposition of the cross is represented as "the devil" or "Satan" (1 Jn 3:8; Lk 10:18).[14]

The theological difficulty to which we have already referred is speaking about the power of darkness in personal and individual terms. We need to recognize the limits of our language at this point. We are speaking symbolically, partially and not definitively.[15] It may be that such language can be seen as personification. But the concept of the devil has a metaphorical and direct force in expressing the relentless power of evil, the overpowering threat to humanity. To substitute any other concept somehow mutes the nature of the threat. The devil concept captures the biblical insight that the highest reaches of sin are not to do with the body so much as with the spirit. The thoroughly evil nature of the devil consists in the fact that here we have sin expressed in pure defiance and pure arrogance.[16]

Problematic though it may be, we struggle to do justice to the reality of this power without recourse to personal language or at least to personification. Even Barth, who chose to speak of evil as Nothingness in order to avoid giving the impression that it had a positive form of being, found it difficult to avoid personal language and affirmed that Nothingness takes form as a "real devil."[17] Reluctant though we should be to dignify the devil with personal language and keen though we may be to qualify it and pack it around with more impersonal talk, when we do this we run the risk of making the power of evil so abstract that we lose its compelling force and clarity.

STEP FIVE

If, then, there is such a power as the devil, the question must now be asked, what is its origin? Religious debate has touched on a variety of areas.

1. The first is that of *metaphysical dualism,* the belief that the conflict between God and Satan is an eternal one. The devil exists as God's "opposite number," with God having slightly the upper hand. The battle wages now one way, now the other. This is the view expressed, as we have seen, by Edwin P. Lewis, although Lewis held open the possibility of an ultimate victory of God over the Adversary. His namesake, C. S. Lewis, was of the opinion that "next to Christianity Dualism is the manliest [sic] and most sensible creed on the market."[18] He said this because, at least, dualism recognizes the element of conflict be-

tween good and evil. But it has a catch in it. Basically, this concept belongs firmly outside the Christian faith. For a Christian view it is a denial of the supremacy of God. It is true to say that the New Testament contains a form of dualism, a conflict between good and evil. But it is a temporary and historical one and not eternal. To make the devil into God's opposite number is to give him a status he does not have and runs the danger of "domesticating" evil by making it part of the eternal order. It therefore loses the sense of the horror and unacceptability of evil.

2. A second point of view is *monism*. It goes to the opposite extreme by perceiving everything that happens, including evil, as directly attributable to the will of God. If evil exists, it is because God has directly willed it. There is no "permissive" will of God that allows things to be what he does not strictly will. Instead, everything exists because God directly wills that it should. There is one cause for everything, namely, the will of God. It is difficult to see how this view avoids making God directly the author and originator of evil, and we are left with immense problems concerning the goodness of God. The monist position has been typical of high Calvinism with its strict theocentrism, which refuses to give room to any lesser cause than God in the affairs of the universe. This position has been able to appeal for support to some biblical texts[19] and to some statements in the works of John Calvin, for instance: "For the first man fell because the Lord had judged it to be expedient; why he so judged is hidden from us. . . . Accordingly, man falls according as God's providence ordains, but he falls by his own fault."[20] To take the monist position would question God's hostility to evil.

3. A third option, then, would be *agnosticism* on the basis that Scripture does not speak to this particular issue, or if it does, it does so only in peripheral texts not easy to interpret. Emil Brunner, for instance, is strong in his acceptance of the reality of the devil because at the center

of the biblical revelation, especially in the life and cross of Jesus, this is to be perceived. But he argues that in the Bible the power of darkness is simply there. We do well not to speculate on its origin, since this is left opaque. The existence of the devil is accepted but left undefined and unaccounted for.[21] There is real point to this. In the prologue to John's Gospel, in the great cascade of divine truth that flows there, having been introduced to the Word through whom all things were made, we are introduced without explanation or warning to the darkness: "The light shines in the darkness and the darkness did not overcome it" (Jn 1:5). The darkness is an unexplained given. With the appearance of the Son of God we also have, without explanation, the appearance of the opposition.

4. The preferred option among Christian thinkers has been that of locating evil in the misuse of a *creaturely freedom*. The church has argued for the freedom of human creatures and has associated evil with the consequent ability to contradict the will of God and declare autonomy. From an early date Christian thinkers have posited a focus of misusable freedom in a transcendent dimension, which is then transposed to the human. Humanity is not the originator of evil but has become implicated in an existing rebellion of a spiritual, suprahuman power responsible for self-generated sin.

STEP SIX

With this suggestion we address the doctrine traditionally known as the "fall of angels," the idea of a precreation, angelic catastrophe. We noted Origen's expression of the doctrine. It occurs first in Tertullian (A.D. c. 160/70-c. 215/20)[22] and finds normative exposition in Augustine (A.D. 354-430).[23] This is a concept that Barth decisively excluded, despite using language reminiscent of it.[24] He rejected the thought that angels could fall because he denied freedom to them. Their existence was identical with their obedience. They lacked autonomy and therefore the possibility of rebellion. Brunner likewise finds fault with the doctrine, seeing no direct scriptural basis for it. The idea of a fall of angels exists for him only on the fringe of the biblical testimony: it is a relic of Persian religion and does not belong to the center of Christian faith. Moreover it has proven to be a happy hunting ground for the imaginations of the fanatical.[25]

The force of these criticisms needs to be felt. In that the Bible speaks of an angelic fall, it does so obliquely and on the margins. The texts concerned are problematic.[26] The Old Testament passages appealed to, Ezekiel 28:1-17 and Isaiah 14:12-21, can only be cited indirectly since their direct reference is to identifiable human persons.[27] They prove what is required of them only if their meaning is assumed in advance on other grounds. It is more likely that they are heightened descriptions of historical persons rather than attempts to describe the origin of Satan.[28] It takes a major leap of biblical interpretation to refer them to a transcendental personage.

The New Testament texts are more substantial, but even so are elusive. Jude 6 speaks of "angels who did not keep their positions of authority but abandoned their own home." 2 Peter 2:4 refers to the fact that "God did not spare angels when they sinned but sent them to hell." If we accept Jude 6 as teaching concerning an angelic fall, are we also bound to accept the account in verse 9 about Michael disputing with the devil about the body of Moses, or verse 14 about Enoch's prophecies? Neither incident is found in the Old Testament but belongs to Jewish extrabiblical literature. Jude is using known Jewish traditions to illustrate his point rather than laying down authoritative teaching.

Second Peter 2:4 is also problematic. The "angels that sinned" appear to be the heavenly beings in Genesis 6:1-14 who lusted after earthly women. The fate of these angels became a subject of speculation in Jewish thought.[29] If so, these angels fell after the creation of humankind and not before it. It may be that these are references to known tradition meant simply to illustrate the writer's theme of the danger of disobedience rather than disclose information concerning a fall of angels.

We need to be cautious before grounding a doctrine of the fall of angels on uncertain exegesis. There is considerable wisdom in retreating into agnosticism with Brunner at this point. Yet it is significant that he, while dismissing the doctrine, nevertheless goes on to speak of Satan as the point of origin and self-generation of evil.[30] Whatever obscurity surrounds the texts, there are also *theological* (in contrast to *exegetical*) reasons for moving toward the concept of an angelic fall.

The concept of the angelic catastrophe locates the origin of evil within the created sphere. Evil is not God's creation but neither can it exist independently of God. Therefore evil must arise from within the creation. It comes from a deliberate misuse of creaturely freedom initially on a transcendent, spiritual level and then on the human plane. We may agree with Barth that evil has no honorable ontological status, but it may have an ontological *ground* in the freedom of humans and angels.[31] It may be parasitical, but it is not passive. It is forceful and dynamic in its own negative way. That evil has its origin in the created sphere is implied by Colossians 1:16—which understands Christ as the origin of both visible and invisible realities—and Romans 8:28-29—which brackets the principalities and powers that might seek to separate us from the love of God among created things.

Evil is not therefore an inevitable part of the structure of things but an aberration within the creation. Barth denied the possibility of such a fall on the basis of his angelology, and to admit the possibility of such an event would deny the understanding of angels he has articulated. But he has no substantial biblical grounds for depriving angels of the kind of being and freedom that would make it possible for them to rebel. It is possible to conceive of angelic powers having their own way of being and some degree of autonomy sufficient for there to have been an aberration. Such an act would deprive angelic powers of their true existence and would cause them to exist only in a negative and chaotic form, feeding parasitically on the good and ordered creation. The concept of Nothingness expresses well what an angelic power might become once it departed from obedience to God. It would exist in contradiction to God, deprived of validity, existing as a negative and malevolent spiritual agency wholly given over to evil and to the thwarting of God's purpose. Barth himself suggests as much when he says that an angel that behaved unangelically would resemble a demon:

> Although he is a creature, and an exemplary and perfect creature, his task as such has simply been to come and then to go again, to pass by. He would be a lying spirit, a demon, if he were to tarry, directing attention and love and honour and even perhaps adoration for himself and enticing man to enter into dealings with fellowship with himself instead of through him into dealings with God.[32]

A further weakness of Barth's view is that it is difficult for it to explain the biblical understanding of an evil strategy that posits some degree of deliberate, malevolent purpose within the power of darkness.[33] The apostle Paul proclaimed, "We are not ignorant of his designs" (2 Cor 2:11; Eph 6:11), and this sense of agency must count for something. An angelic fall might make this intelligible if it identifies the factor of intelligence in this evil power.

STEP SEVEN

An angelic rebellion may be a point of origin for evil, but it does not explain how and why it should take place. We are here posed with a genuine difficulty. Were angelic beings to rebel against God, we have no explanation as to why they should wish to do this. Wink's suggestion that Satan, in his proper mode of being, was to fulfill the task of proving and testing humanity by representing the choices that were alternatives to God's will, and that his fall came when he overstepped the mark in his role of *agent provocateur*, is an intriguing one. Satan's fall would be seen as going too far in a direction in which he was already set. The impulse to overstep the mark becomes more comprehensible on this understanding. However, the Bible supplies us with little on the basis of which to speak with authority in this realm.

STEP EIGHT

While questioning Barth's concept of Nothingness, it does illuminate us in a further step. Evil is inexplicable, and yet the possibility of it exists as the negative side of a positive world. It exists by mimicry, contradiction and distortion. It exists as discreativity dependent on God's creativity. Evil is self-generating, but it is not, strictly speaking, self-creating. The power of darkness is not able to create anything. It can only distort what already exists. As C. S. Lewis has it, "Goodness is, so to speak, itself: badness is only spoiled goodness. And there must be something good before it can be spoiled. . . . Evil is a parasite, not an original thing."[34]

The possibility of evil exists by virtue of God's creative work but only as its reverse side and denial, as that which God excludes from his own work. Evil functions as a form of antimatter, a cosmic black hole warring against that which is created and sustained by God, and yet only existing by virtue of it. God has created a world in which this possibility exists of necessity. Barth is correct in saying that God's creative "Yes!" implies a "No!" but not in saying that God's implied "No!" actually *creates* or gives rise to evil. A possibility does not create a reality corresponding to it, but it does allow that malevolence will arise within creation and give actuality to the possibility of evil. God's creative action of necessity produces the possibility of evil, but it takes other agencies to turn that possibility into actuality.

STEP NINE

God, in creating this world, made it with the possibility to go astray inherent within it. This implies that he has built into it a certain "freedom" over against himself—and that this freedom is of the essence of what it means for humans to be human and for the world to be the world. Because evil cannot have been unforeseen it must also follow that God is not without responsibility. He is not the author of evil, but he is the author of creation and of the risk inherent in it. As we shall see, the significance of the cross of Jesus is that the one who suffers most because of sin is God, and by his own action in the cross evil is actually overcome. At the cross, Jesus Christ overcame the power of the devil. This victory comes from God alone.[35]

Step Ten

The fact that on the cross evil was overcome does not mean that the conflict with the powers of darkness does not continue. There is a fierce conflict yet to be waged, and the worst of the conflict may be yet to come. Nevertheless, the decisive victory that has already been achieved awaits its fulfillment and consummation. Many years ago Oscar Cullmann applied to this the celebrated analogy of D-Day and V-Day. When the Allied forces, in the struggle to liberate occupied Europe, landed on the Normandy beaches, they won the decisive victory. From that point on the result of the war was a foregone conclusion. Yet it was some time before victory was finally proclaimed in Europe. In the intervening period the battle was at its fiercest as a cornered enemy fought to the bitter end. So, Cullmann wrote:

> In the time between the resurrection and the Parousia of Christ [the angelic powers] are, so to speak, bound as to a rope which can be more or less lengthened, so that those among them who show tendencies to emancipation can have the illusion that they are releasing themselves from their bond with Christ, while in reality, by this striving which here and there appears, they only show once more their original demonic character; they cannot, however, actually set themselves free. Their power is only appar-

ent. The church has so much more the duty to stand against them, in view of the fact that it knows that their power is only apparent and that in reality Christ has already conquered all demons.[36]

Earlier on we were at pains to stress the irrationality of evil, our inability to fit it neatly into a system that makes sense. Now we are also able to assert that because God is the Lord of heaven and earth he is able to make even this senseless and meaningless evil serve his own purpose. This is not because evil has its own hidden meaning but because, against its own will, God is able to make it serve a greater meaning. The cross is the supreme example of how God is able to master evil and cause even that to serve his good purpose.

TOWARD COHERENCE

Robert Cook argued that there are logically only four possibilities for locating the origin of evil: in a created entity beyond our universe; in God; in the structure of created reality; or in the human race. He excluded God and expressed a cautious preference for the third option, while acknowledging that the preference has been for the first in the Christian tradition. In his assessment of Cook, Tom Noble turns his attention to the neglected fourth option. He draws attention to the fact that in Genesis, a book concerned with origins, the human fall is center stage.[37] An angelic fall is totally absent, as it is from the teaching of the apostle Paul, whose definitive interpretation of Genesis clearly identifies the fall of humankind at the center.

Sin and death came into the world through the one man, "Adam" (Rom 5:12-14). "Adam" therefore defines the human condition and history until it is redefined in a second Adam, Christ (Rom 5:15-21). If indeed the fall into sin is an act of stupidity rather than intelligence, a product of arrogance rather than imagination, it is credible to locate it as an act of human beings. In the light of the weight given to the human fall, Noble advances that suprahuman evil be seen as a projection and consequence of the human fall and not vice versa.[38] What follows works out from this central point.

Counting against this construct is the detail that the serpent acts as a tempter in Genesis 3 and therefore precedes human beings. However, Genesis itself does not identify the serpent as the devil but only as a wild animal. Is it possible that this could represent something else? We are helped here by Cook's third option concerning the structure of creation. God creates a chaos and then from the chaos establishes an ordered world. Yet the creation is pressured, according to Cook, by "the urge back into formless, lifeless, meaningless chaos."[39] This accords with the Hebrew tendency to see in the chaos of the sea the remnants of the still-threatening primeval chaos and to depict this as a sea-serpent or a dragon.[40]

In light of this, is the symbol of the serpent in Genesis 3 significant? Humankind is born into a testing environment where the collapse back into chaos is a threat to the whole creation. This threat precedes humanity. Cook is inclined to see the chaos as itself evil, presumably precisely because it is chaotic. My own inclination is to see it as the occasion for evil rather than as evil in itself. Of itself it is a stage in God's creative work.

To develop this I draw attention to Reinhold Niebuhr's compelling analysis of temptation and sin. For Niebuhr the "internal precondition" of sin is *anxiety*. Human beings come into the world as *finite* creatures who are capable of thoughts of *infinity*. This creates a state of anxiety as they are caught between finiteness and freedom. They fear the abyss of meaningless. This situation is not of itself evil because anxiety can be resolved through trust in God. Fearing insecurity, however, and interpreting their situation falsely, human beings adopt another strategy. They find security in pride, in self-exaltation maintained by holding power over others. Alternatively they escape their insecurity through immersing themselves in sensuality. Sin comes into being therefore when, in people's finite existence, they perceive and respond to their security being threatened.[41]

Within this analysis Niebuhr draws attention approvingly to the notion of the devil as a fallen angel: "To believe that there is a devil is to believe that there is a principle or force of evil antecedent to any evil human action."[42] He unravels this mystery as: "sin posits itself."[43] This means that in order for the devil to sin there would have to be a way in which "sin posits itself" first to the devil, and it makes sense to believe that sin posits itself to humanity in a situation of anxiety. The serpent therefore represents this anxiety, interpreted not as an occasion for trust in God but for the displacement of God. It is a temptation and a testing, and perhaps for this reason, it merits the retrospective interpretation in Revelation 12:9 of the serpent in the Garden as "that ancient serpent, who is called the Devil and Satan." Notice however that this reference could equally (or also) be to the image of the chaos as a sea serpent.

Might it be possible to see in this analysis the transition of the *idea* of Satan from "holy sifter" to that of "unholy adversary"? Human beings exist in a context that tests (sifts) them. The appropriate response is trust in God. Nonetheless, it is not the context that is evil but the actual response of self-exaltation made to it. Out of this negative and godless response there comes the tragic history of hostility toward the Creator, of which the devil is the supreme expression.

A crucial divergence of interpretation emerges at this point between seeing the devil as an ontological reality over and beyond humankind, preceding humanity in a fall, or as a construct or projection to emerge as a consequence of the human fall. In exploring the second alternative Noble shows sympathy for Robert Cook's inclination "to view Satan as the mythic personification of human society arising out of collective human evil, the supreme archetype from the collective unconscious of the wickedness of."[44] These words build on Walter Wink:

> Satan thus becomes the symbol of the spirit of an entire society alienated from God, the great system of mutual support in evil, the spirit of persistent self-deification blown large, the image of unredeemed humanity's

collective life. . . . Satan is the real interiority of a society that idolatrously pursues its own enhancement as the highest good. Satan is the spirituality of an epoch, the peculiar constellation of alienation, greed, inhumanity, oppression, and entropy that characterizes a specific period of history as a consequence of human decisions to tolerate and even further such a state of affairs.[45]

In this way we can address the question of the ontological status of the devil. Of himself he has none, but he does have an *ontological ground* or a point at which he might emerge in the existence of humankind. He is the construct, albeit a real one, of fallen society. Without a created ontology he is nonetheless real, but in the same way that a vacuum or a black hole or death itself are real. A vacuum is intensely powerful even though it consists of sheer emptiness. A black hole is a collapsed star unobservable apart from its impact on other stars and its capacity to suck matter into itself. Death is not itself an ontological substance but the very negation of all life by which we are continually harried. Noble comments:

> this speculation about supra-human evil is deficient if it understands Satan as *merely* a mythical projection or personification. Rather, we would have to conceive of a real and objective supreme power of evil which draws its reality and strength from the perverted corporate unconscious of humanity. Some kind of symbiotic relationship may be posited in which the powers of evil draw their strength and perverse vitality and truly demonic energy (possibly indeed their very being?) from human wickedness, while we human beings in our sin are enthralled to powers beyond our control.[46]

Satan language therefore is a "mythic" personification of collective human evil, but it is the language alone that is mythic, not the reality. Noble finds significant biblical support here in Paul's discussion of pagan gods in 1 Corinthians 8 and 10. They have no real existence (8:4), but there are many gods and many lords (8:5) in the sense that people believe in them and this investment of belief gives them a paradoxical but powerful reality.[47]

How does this approach impinge on the discussion of a "personal" devil? I have previously pointed to the difficulty of applying personal language to the devil. The issue recurs in thinking about redemption. If we are to believe that God's "compassion is over all that he has made" (Ps 145:8), that in Christ "all things in heaven and on earth were made, things visible and invisible," and that "through him God was pleased to reconcile to himself all things, whether on earth or in heaven" (Col 1:16, 20), must we not further conclude that it is at least possible for the devil to be redeemed if his existence is that of a rebellious creature? This exact conclusion was drawn first of all by Origen (A.D. c. 185-c. 254). Although the devil's purposes and hostile will would perish, his substance, which is God's creation, would be saved since there is nothing that cannot be healed by its Creator.[48]

Paul Ricoeur put it differently: "I know not what Satan is, who Satan is, or even whether he is Someone. For if he were someone, it would be necessary to intercede for him."[49] There is no suggestion in Scripture that the devil has such a future, in fact quite the reverse (Rev 20:10). This issue is resolved if we follow Noble's construct, since according to it there is no "substance," no created ontology to be saved. If Satan exists as a projection of the corporate spirit of fallen humanity the day of redemption will spell the end of the devil and the demonic. They will simply cease. Must we go on to say that personal language applied to the devil is personification and no more?

The train of thought we are pursuing points in this direction. In *The Screwtape Letters* Screwtape, the senior devil, breaks off his letter to Wormwood on one occasion with the words, "In the heat of composition I find that I have inadvertently allowed myself to assume the form of a large centipede. I am accordingly dictating the rest of the letter to my secretary." The letter is finished and signed by Toadpipe.[50] The moment is an instructive one. It suggests that the nature of evil is not ordered rationality but chaos. Evil, being inherently deceptive, *masquerades* as something it is not and yet cannot keep itself from collapsing into chaos. It may be that any pretense of evil to personhood remains simply this, a pretense, at best a personification.

However, there is also a sense in which all human personhood is *constructed*, enabled to come to be via the relationships that surround us from birth and continue through life. Is there a way therefore in which, out of the unconscious, fallen human collective psyche the devil and even the demons might be constructed as hypostases? Noble continues his analysis of evil with some intriguing, if necessarily speculative, thinking.

He is keen to deny that the devil is personal in the way that this might be true of human beings. If we follow a trinitarian understanding of human persons as being defined by relationships of love we cannot in any way attribute this to the devil. This does not however preclude the possibility of thinking of the devil as "a malevolent intelligence, willing, acting, and knowing, but totally lacking in personal feeling or sympathy, and obsessed with self-aggrandisement."[51] The devil, although a projection out from fallen humanity, is not merely this but possesses a way of being, agency, even if this way of being is

> inherently deception, falseness, delusion, vanity, emptiness and pretence. It appears to be what it is not. And this is not just what it does: it is what it is. Since it is inherently deceptive, and indeed self-deceptive, it is consequently quite impossible to give a structured, meaningful account of it. It is the surd element in creation. It cannot be analysed or accounted for in structured discourse, for it is the very opposer, the enemy and denial of the Logos of God. It can only be referred to by image and myth.[52]

Noble draws attention in the course of his discussion to the influential definition of the philosopher Boethius (A.D. c. 480-c. 524) of personhood as "the individual substance of rational nature" and argues that, while this falls woefully short of a trinitarian understanding of person-hood, it is a minimalist definition that the devil might be able to fulfill insofar as he is "an agent able to think, to know, to will and to act."[53] It is a kind of personal identity but not one that can be understood as in any way on par with the fuller personal being of humans. Also referring critically to Boethius, Robert Jenson makes a similar point. Paraphrasing Boethius' definition as "an individual entity endowed with intellect," he sees Satan fulfilling this minimalist definition: "It is his ontological particularity to satisfy Boethius' definition and nevertheless lack person-hood. There is doubtless some connection between the problem of demonology and the much-debated problem of machine intelligence—as much popular literature perceives."[54]

This is no complete solution, but it may offer a direction along which a solution might lie. The devil possesses a much-reduced and essentially malevolent way of being, which to dignify as personhood would be vastly to overrate. There is one area that may be overlooked by Cook's and Noble's directions of thought: it concerns the question of pre-human pain and suffering. The myth of a fall of angels has been called into account for the existence of evident suffering in creation even before the appearance of human beings. Such evil, if such it should be described, cannot be accounted for by means of the human fall. In the next chapter we give some consideration to these issues among others.

CHAPTER FIVE

THE PROBLEM OF EVIL

No greater challenge is posed to Christian belief than that which is normally called "the problem of evil." This is true on both philosophical and personal levels. There are few who pass through life unscathed. Most of us experience, at one time or another, life's "strange mutations."[1] It can deal the cruelest of blows through a painful illness, a sudden death, a tragic accident. It is not unusual for us to ask the question, why does God allow this? People will often excuse themselves from actively believing in God on the basis that they have "seen too much in life." What they are saying is that a simple, hopeful belief in a loving God seems too naive a faith in such a complex world.

Those who find such a faith difficult may simply be using the world's suffering as an excuse for avoiding God. But it would be insensitive or stupid people who did not feel themselves questioning when faced with blatant and senseless suffering. The twentieth century revealed more of this than previous centuries, not only because we are better informed, but also because of the vast amount of inhumanity perpetrated by individuals, ideologies and states. The horrendous slaughter of the First World War exploded the optimistic hopes for the perfecting of the human race held by previous generations. The death camps of the Second World War, the nuclear devastation of Hiroshima and Nagasaki, the fire storms of Hamburg and Dresden, to say nothing of the countless smaller wars and acts of atrocity that have continued unabated ever since, may very well cause us to ask whether the God of the universe is a loving Father or a cosmic sadist.

Nowhere is this question put more movingly or with greater moral authority than in the writings of the 1986 Nobel Prize winner, Eli Wiesel. In his book *Night*, Wiesel records his teenage years spent in the concentration camps at Auschwitz and Buchenwald. The book is dedicated to his parents and his little sister, Tzapora. He had seen his mother, sister and all his family disappear into the ovens. His father was to die more slowly. The story is told with infinitely deep sadness. From his earliest days as the child of a devout Jewish family, Wiesel had loved God with a profound and rare instinct. But for this child, the concentration camp was to destroy the God he had known.

> Never shall I forget that night, the first night in the camp, which has turned my life into one long night, seven times cursed and seven times sealed. Never shall I forget that smoke. Never shall I forget the little faces of the children, whose bodies I saw turned into wreaths of smoke beneath a silent blue sky. Never shall I forget those flames which consumed my faith forever. Never shall I forget that nocturnal silence which deprived me, for all eternity, of the desire to live. Never shall I forget those moments which murdered my God and my soul and turned my dreams to dust. Never shall I forget these things, even if I am condemned to live as long as God Himself, Never.[2]

In another place he describes an experience that must have been shared by thousands:

> Once, New Year's Day had dominated my life. I knew that my sins grieved the Eternal; I implored his forgiveness. Once, I had believed profoundly that upon one solitary deed of mine, one solitary prayer, depended the salvation of the world. This day I had ceased to plead. I was no longer capable of lamentation. On the contrary, I felt very strong. I was the accuser, God the accused. My eyes were open and I was alone—terribly alone in a world without God and without man, without love or mercy. I had ceased to be anything but ashes, yet I felt myself to be stronger than the Almighty, to whom my life had been tied for so long. I stood amid that praying congregation, observing it like a stranger.[3]

Who among us is able to dismiss such experience or such questions as trivial? The Christian belief in God has something to say, but any answer must be hard won, for it cannot be lightly given.

The personal experience of suffering gives rise to the philosophical question concerning the existence of God. The argument against the existence of God was cogently stated by the eighteenth-century Scottish philosopher David Hume: "Is he willing to prevent evil, but not able? then he is impotent. Is he able, but not willing? then he is malevolent. Is he both able and willing? whence then is evil?"[4] The problem is posed here in terms of a logical dilemma that calls the existence of God into question. The bulk of this chapter is concerned with a response to this dilemma. Toward its conclusion we will return to the personal dimensions of the issue.

First, it may be helpful to outline several distinctions in the form evil takes. There is first of all *metaphysical evil*. By this we mean that form of evil that transcends individual human minds and causes us to look for a transhuman source.[5] A second form of evil is that of *moral evil*, that is, evil that can be attributed to the misuse of humankind's own moral freedom. A third form is that of *physical* or *passive evil*, by which is meant those forms of suffering and destruction that are to be found in the physical universe and cannot be directly attributed to sinful behavior.

RESPONSES TO THE PROBLEM OF EVIL

How then have thinkers responded to the dilemma posed by the problem of evil? A variety of possible positions are here set out.

Evil as illusion. One way of escaping from the dilemma is to deny the existence of evil and to argue that it is an illusion. This is characteristic of Hindu religion, which affirms ultimate reality to be both one and good, and so that which appears in this world to be many and evil is illusion. This monism (understanding the world in terms of one single ground or cause) has no room for any kind of dualism (the belief that two opposing principles are at work). A modern form of this kind of belief in the West is Christian Science, which understands evil as a false perception, an error of the mortal mind. Sin, sickness and death do not exist in reality.

The questions posed by this attitude are considerable. Why does the illusion appear so real if it does not exist? And if the illusion feels so real, what practical difference does it make to view it as an illusion? Or to quote Edward Lear:

> A certain faith-healer of Deal
> Asserted: "Pain is not real!"
> "Then pray tell me why,"
> Came the patient's reply,
> "When I sit on a pin
> And puncture my skin,
> Do I hate what I fancy I feel?"[6]

The concept of illusion does not help to resolve the problem of evil since it raises too many questions about itself.

God as finite. A second approach to the dilemma is to alter the premises on which the argument is based. If God is good, but not almighty, then we have an adequate explanation of why he does not deal with evil. He does not because he can not. God also is the victim of evil in the world, as are we. This of course is the solution posed by the idea of an ultimate dualism. God's power is not absolute and therefore he is not in full control of evil. He too is struggling against it. A view that is similar in this respect is represented by process theology, certain versions of which (not all) view God as finite and limited. Process theology sees reality not as a series of static objects but as a process of becoming. God is in the world luring it toward harmony and the good. Evil consists of incompatible factors that need to be accepted and then transformed into the process that moves toward the good. God is involved in the process of struggling with evil, and humankind is called to cooperate with God in this struggle upward and forward.

Some aspects of this way of thinking are of considerable value, but grave problems are caused by the concept of a finite God and the view that God can absorb evil into himself in his ongoing process of becoming. It is difficult to see how these themes in process thought can be squared with biblical faith. On a more ironic level, we might feel we have enough problems of our own without having to help God with his as well.

Evil as good. A third response to the problem of evil will be exposed to the same kind of criticism made of process theology. This denies the absolutely evil nature of evil and argues that it is really a disguised form of the good. It will prove necessary to spend some time on this response since the issues it raises are complex and our discussion of it will not be exhausted in this section.

The creative voice in this context belongs to the philosopher Gottfried von Leibniz (1646-1716) who sought to refute the argument by maintaining that this is the best of all possible worlds. The world is moving toward perfection. It is not yet perfect, but in achieving perfection, the evil aspects of it are essential ingredients in the whole.[7] The conclusion to be drawn from this is that evil cannot really be regarded as evil since it is actually serving a good purpose. It is the means of moral growth through which perfection is being achieved and therefore even the pain of life can be seen to serve a good purpose.

This is similar to process theology in the perception that evil which is accepted and built upon may actually be the means of progress toward the good. The fact that good has its opposite in evil serves to enhance the good, to show it up by contrast and to bring out its true goodness. This operates in our own lives. There are many unpleasant and difficult experiences that we would not choose to undergo but that are thrust on us so that we have no choice. These trials are difficult at the time, but it is through them that we grow in character. Suffering does sometimes produce growth in human development when it is accepted without bitterness and yielded up to God. Looking back we may say about many such experiences that we have benefited from them, we are better people as a result. Furthermore, this is confirmed by Scripture, which speaks of God's painful discipline that later "produces a harvest of righteousness and peace for those who have been trained by it" (Heb 12:11) and affirms that "in all things God works for the good of those who love him" (Rom 8:28). Perhaps, after all, evil is not really all that evil but simply a disguised form of the good!

A significant contribution to this discussion has been made by John A. Sanford, an Episcopalian priest and psychoanalyst. Sanford develops insights from the works of the pioneering psychologist Carl Jung and argues that to understand evil helps us better to understand God.[8] Evil has a very positive role to play in the development of individuals. It is the shadow side of reality that belongs as of right to creation. As the person without a shadow does not exist physically so we cannot exist as true persons without a shadow. What we judge evil depends on the perspective from which we speak. Only the ultimate, divine perspective would enable us to see the positive role of evil within universal human history.[9] Specifically, evil helps the development of human nature by stimulating its capacity for moral feeling. It acts as a catalyst in enabling growth toward individual wholeness. The shadow is necessary for the growth of the human personality.[10] Far from being wholly evil it is, like Mephistopheles in Goethe's *Faust*, "Part of a power that would / Alone work evil but engenders good."[11]

There is considerable force to this argument and much that is attractive. We will return to it in another form. There are echoes here of Walter Wink's concept of the devil as God's servant, his "holy sifter." Yet caution needs to be exercised before we go too far too fast down this road. Sanford himself, in expounding the thought of Jung, sees the danger. Jung criticized the traditional concept of evil because it belittled evil and thereby, in his opinion, belittled the good.

There is no white without black, no right without left, no above without below, no warm without cold, no truth without error, no light without darkness etc. If evil is an illusion God is necessarily illusory too.[12]

Such thinking causes Jung to argue that evil must not only be necessary for human beings but also for God. The Christian doctrine of God lacks, he considers, the necessary dimension of a dark side. In place of the doctrine of the Trinity he advocates the concept of Quaternity, in which the Adversary takes his place along with Father, Son and Spirit within the Godhead.[13]

What is happening here? First, evil has been declared to be no longer truly evil. Second, the idea of an ultimate and radical hostility between God and evil has been lost sight of. Third, the devil has been enthroned within the Godhead as a divine person. There is a logical progression to this: once the irreducible and unqualified wickedness of evil has been lost sight of, it is not long before the devil takes his place and reigns in divine splendor. As we will see, the concept of the shadow side has something to commend it but not along the lines suggested by Jung. Evil cannot be seen as part of the good, or even as necessary to it, since to do that is to make evil itself partly good.

Evil as necessary. We turn to the view that evil is the product of the misuse of God-given freedom. The possibility that free beings might choose evil rather than good is a necessary part of human freedom. This position is known as the free will defense. It counters Hume's objection that God cannot be both omnipotent and loving in view of the fact of evil by seeing it as an oversimplification of the actual case. God is both omnipotent and loving and as such has created free beings. As it is logically impossible for God to create a free being who automatically does what is right (in this case there would be no freedom), he has therefore introduced into the creation a freedom that is neither conditioned nor predetermined. Humankind has relative freedom toward God and is able to disobey and resist him. This does not compromise the omnipotence of God since omnipotence does not mean that God can do that which is logically impossible. He cannot create a square circle or a color that is simultaneously black and white. These are logical impossibilities, as is the idea of a free being who automatically chooses the right. God might have chosen not to create a world at all or have chosen to create a world populated by sinless robots.

Actually, God has chosen to create a world in which there are free creatures because it is the best possible way toward the kind of world and the kind of people he ultimately desires. This is not inconsistent with the love of God since this is demonstrated in the very freedom he gives to humans. Yet such freedom carries with it great risks, and it is the riskiness of love that means that there is suffering in the world. The free will defense maintains that God is omnipotent, omniscient and wholly good but that it was not within God's power to create a world containing moral good without creating one containing the possibility of moral evil.[14] The risk of evil is a necessary part of free existence and is incompatible with neither the power nor the love of God.

The last paragraph has approached the problem of evil as a logical one. Yet this is not the only way to do so. Much disbelief in God is not a scientifically calculated rejection of the proposition "God exists" but a heartfelt protest against the depth and extent of human suffering. This "protest atheism" rejects the existence of a loving God because the notion seems implausible in the light of the facts. It is not enough to demonstrate the possibility of moral evil as necessarily involved in human freedom. When we are actually faced with human suffering, logical arguments are somewhat hollow. What the Christian faith offers is the belief, not yet provable, that there is "a future good great enough to justify all that has happened on the way to it."[15] And, in view of the amount of suffering, this future will have to be great indeed to outweigh it.

It is this vision of the future that the Bible offers us when it speaks of a restored and healed world in which suffering and sorrow have no place

(Col 1:20; Rev 21:1-4). The model for this confidence is the cross of Christ, which is simultaneously the focus of the worst evil and the greatest good. The powers of darkness beyond and within the human race do their worst and seek to obliterate the embodiment of supreme goodness in a horrific way. The Christ suffers and is rejected. Yet this event is also the greatest revelation of the love of God who by enduring evil in Christ actually overcomes it. It is because of this that Christians can believe that all things can be shaped to fulfill the purpose of God. Evil is not of God and is in no sense good, but God's power is such that even evil can be made ultimately to serve him (Rom 8:28). God is the God who creates out of nothing. This does not make evil less evil and should not lead us to entertain positive ideas about it, but it is a testimony to the power of God who is able to bring good out of evil, just as he was able to create the world out of nothing.

A one-time TV advertisement for *The Guardian* newspaper may help in understanding this. It showed the same scene from three different angles. In the first shot a young man, dressed as a skinhead, runs toward a well-dressed businessman carrying a briefcase, knocking him over. The conclusion the viewer draws is that the skinhead is mugging the businessman with the intention of robbing him. In the second shot the scene is shown from a different angle. This time a car has drawn up behind the skinhead and three beefy-looking men climb out. The skinhead runs toward the businessman and knocks him over. The viewer revises his interpretation and concludes that the skinhead is being chased by plainclothes police and, in his flight, accidentally sends the businessman sprawling. The third shot is taken from above, and this time it is seen that a load is suspended from a crane above the businessman. It is about to slip and to fall on top of the man. What is actually happening is that the skinhead has seen the danger and is running toward the man to push him out of the way and so save his life at the risk of his own. At the end of the commercial the message is that *The Guardian* gives the right perspective on things. Viewers are left repenting of their prejudices!

To understand events correctly we need to have the right perspective on them. We do not yet have the perspective because we are too close to the action. As time passes we gain greater perspective on events. But it is only in the light of the fullness of time that we understand both the meaning of events and the role they have played in the purpose of God. In the light of God's ultimate purpose it will be seen that evil, though immense, is finite, while the good for which God is preparing us is infinite. The ultimate joy will greatly surpass the present sorrow and suffering in the created order. With this faith and hope Christians live in the present, believing that, as God worked through the events of the cross to achieve the reconciliation of humanity to himself, he is working through the events of history toward his final goal of reconciling all things.

THE PROBLEM OF PHYSICAL EVIL

We have not yet exhausted the problem of evil. So far in this book, we have given accounts of metaphysical and moral evil, but what about physical evil? It has often been remarked that, as Freud took the lid off human consciousness and revealed the mass of conflicting drives and emotions in human beings, so Darwin before him took the lid off nature and demonstrated how it was "red in tooth and claw." Suffering is not confined to the human species. The animal creation is aware of pain. It is expressed in the way one species preys on another and in how death and dying are a part of the cycle of creation. Conflict and carnivorousness appear to be normative parts of the animal kingdom. Then there are natural disasters, earthquakes, floods, volcanoes, hurricanes, which cannot be attributed to the moral choices of people in any direct sense. Physical evil poses the question about the nature of the Creator God. If the creation reflects the being of God its Creator, then surely the Creator too must have his dark side, a cruel, sadistic streak? Once more we will survey a number of responses.

The problem is not as bad as it seems. It is possible to exaggerate the problem of pain in relation to the physical universe. The animal kingdom is characterized by cooperation far more than conflict. There are many examples of different species living and functioning harmoniously together. The conflict that does exist serves a useful purpose in that predatory behavior is necessary to prevent decrepit old age or decomposing carcasses. The life of many animals may be short and threatened, but they exist without the kind of anxiety that humans know. Animal pain is real but is not as bad as human beings may imagine. Their nervous systems are less developed than ours and provide a possible anesthetic when wounded. We need to beware of the "pathetic fallacy" that imagines animals to have a human consciousness of their own existence when, in fact, their manner of existence is different from ours—though they can possess great enjoyment of it. Besides, at lower levels of animal life and in the vegetable kingdom, to talk of evil in the way we do becomes meaningless. The problem of physical pain is by no means as great as may be imagined. Even then it must be recognized that pain fulfills a useful purpose. It acts as a warning signal and, indeed, actually highlights the joy of existing.

This reductionist approach to physical evil certainly encourages us to put things in perspective. It is not necessary to see suffering beneath a certain threshold of organic complexity. It can however be objected that in the animal world (and in human beings taken as animals) there are elements that do not easily find explanation. For instance, the onset of cancer is not accompanied by pain as a warning that something is wrong. The process is the other way around, in that cancer begins painlessly and becomes progressively more painful. Such pain serves no useful purpose, and it is this meaningless element that is problematic. Despite these elements it can be argued quite cogently that the nature of much created life is transient. The physical world exists in a process of change where all the units of nature are in flux.

The ongoing life of nature flows, so to speak, through these units, and each of them has its own brief period of individual existence before the elements composing it are reclaimed, only to be organised again into new forms within the larger whole.[16]

This account of the nature of the creation leaves us with a world in which there are cooperation and conflict and which is both impressive and fierce. Yet such a world is clean and noble in its own way with the conflict fulfilling a higher purpose in which the life of each unit is yielded up into the greater whole. In the evolutionary process this is salutary in that it creates resilience and strength through struggle. Life grows strong exactly because it is contested. The difficulty comes in accounting for the forms of pain that cannot be made to fit into this scheme and are seemingly without meaning.

Physical evil is the result of moral evil. Another attempt to account for physical evil attributes it directly or indirectly to human sin. This is plainly true in the disruptive effect that human beings can have on the environment. The callous disregard for creation that often accompanies the desire to exploit the world's resources is certainly an increasingly significant factor in an industrialized world. It is even true that some disease is the result of human choices to live in certain ways. We are intimately linked to our environment. But traditional accounts of the Fall have pointed to the fact that humankind was created as the vice-regent of creation. The command was given to rule over the earth (Gen 1:26). Human beings are the high point of creation with all things placed under them (Ps 8:6-8). The Fall resulting from rebellion against God means that this position has been lost. Instead of ruling as stewards under God, human beings are now alienated from the Creator and the creation. Instead of existing in harmony with it, the creation is now hostile. The ground is cursed and brings forth thorns and thistles (Gen 3:17-19, 23-24).

It is argued that the Fall of the human race led to a fall of creation because the whole of creation is bound up with human rulership of it. The physical evil we see does not properly belong to the creation but is there because humankind, in its fall, has taken creation with it. According to Calvin, Adam by his original sin "perverted the whole order of nature in heaven and on earth."[17] The conflict, cruelty and pain in creation must therefore be attributed directly to human sin. In support of this view, a number of significant biblical details may be mustered.

- Genesis 1—3 clearly portrays the creation of a good world. Genesis 1 gives an account of seven days in which God created the world, pronouncing over it that it is good at the end of each stage. When the work was completed with the creation of humanity he pronounced it "very good" (Gen 1:31), and he and the creation entered into a Sabbath rest of blessedness. The idyllic scene was disrupted by the rebellion and disobedience at which point mankind and creation went wrong.

  The theodicy of Christian theology, building upon the scriptural testimony, defends the goodness of God by setting the free decision of the first man as the factor "bringing death into the world and all our woe."[18]

- Paul's teaching concerning the first Adam in Romans 5:12-14 appears to confirm this picture. Here, according to Paul, sin and its consequence, death, have entered the world through Adam's sin. It is concluded that the creation prior to Adam was free from death.

- Further confirmation is found in Romans 8:20, which speaks of the creation being "subjected to frustration, not by its own choice, but by the will of the one who subjected it." By this subjection, creation has entered into a "bondage of decay." Understood within the context of the two previous points, it is possible to take this to mean that through human sin the world has become subject to death and to the cycle of decay. Although the one who subjects the world to frustration is usually considered to be God himself, it is in view of sin that this takes place.

According to this view, then, physical evil is directly attributable to moral evil, and God himself is cleared of responsibility. But there are problems. The chief among them is the problem posed by theories of evolution. An evolutionary understanding of human development holds that, far from death and decay entering into the physical world through Adam's sin, they are inherent in nature itself, functioning as an essential part of the evolutionary process. Furthermore, evolutionists would argue that the evidence of pain and suffering in the animal kingdom prior to human emergence on earth is unambiguously clear in the fossil records. To maintain this particular interpretation of Scripture it is necessary to construct an alternative scientific model that would be in harmony with the biblical interpretation followed. This has not been convincingly achieved, in my judgment, despite the loud protests of creationists to the contrary.

Further difficulties attend this view. A world totally free of death and decay is one that would be radically different from the world we presently know. A world constructed on a different pattern ceases to bear any resemblance to a world in which, for instance, the seasonal cycle of growth, death and decay is not only fundamental but also in its own way beautiful. Indeed, Genesis does not suggest a world that is perfect and not prone to decay. Adam and Eve are placed in the Garden to subdue and manage it, presumably because it had the capacity to get out of hand. Furthermore, the significant detail of Genesis 3:22, where God said to guard against eating of the tree of life, suggests that Adam and Eve were not inherently immortal. Immortality was a possibility open to them rather than an inherent quality they forfeited.

If this was so about humankind it becomes necessary to think about the animal kingdom as prone to death and dying. In fact, this interpretation is quite consistent with both Genesis 3:3 and Romans 5:12, where it is the death of men and women that is the result of sin, not the entry of death and decay into the physical world. It seems far more likely that

96

death and decay are actually part of the processes of the good creation. Everyone's body can be understood as being subject to death in the physical sense—yet with the opportunity of receiving immortality through maintaining fellowship with God. In this case the death that enters through sin is not physical cessation of existence but the death in alienation and anxiety that is characteristic of humanity out of fellowship with God. Were men and women not sinners, their physical life might well have come to its natural end, not in death as we now know it, but in a transition to glory such as that legendarily experienced by Enoch (Gen 5:24).

In the light of these difficulties there is a variant of the view that Adam's sin is the cause of the fall of the physical universe. The Fall of Adam not only affected creation prospectively—in the sense that a transition from an original to an imperfect creation took place in time through Adam's sin—but also affected creation retrospectively. The Fall of Adam may therefore be regarded as the cause of the frustrated nature of creation both before and after the actual time of Adam's sin.[19] This view is represented by Bruce Milne, who sees a link between sin and suffering, in that

> all our sinning flows from Adam's primal act of folly which subjected the whole universe prospectively and retrospectively to the forces of decay and cosmic wickedness, and hence to the possibility of suffering and tragedy.[20]

This is a subtle approach to the issue and argues that Romans 8:20, which speaks of the subjection of creation to frustration (presumably by God), does not specify when this took place. It could be the case that God subjected the world prior to Adam's existence but in view of the forthcoming sin he foresaw. What happens in sequence in time may be deemed to happen simultaneously to the eternal God and therefore, viewed from God's point of view, there need be no sequential fall of creation, but nevertheless one that is consequent on humanity's foreseen sin.

Physical evil is caused by the devil's fall, not humanity's. Genesis 3 suggests, as previously noted, that there was already, before human beings came into existence, an element in the creation that was fallen, represented in Eden by the serpent. Here we have an indication that human sin, potent though it may be, nevertheless needs to be understood within the wider context of a power working in opposition to God. We return to the notion of metaphysical evil, the idea that there was an aberration in creation prior to the human Fall. We discussed this in terms of a fall of angels, a rebellion against God of spiritual beings created by him. In the terms of the free will defense, such creatures, like humans, are free. If this is accepted it is possible to think of physical evil as the result of the activity of such powers within creation prior to the appearance of human beings. Natural evil may be attributed to the free action of nonhuman "people." In favor of this point of view it may be noted that on one occasion, at least, Jesus attributed disease directly to Satan and recognized his agency in this regard (Lk 13:16).

C. S. Lewis argued that, since it is no longer possible to trace animal suffering to the Fall of Adam, it could be attributed to a satanic corruption, but he limits this to the animal sphere. The vegetable kingdom may also exhibit the tendency for plant to prey on plant, but this he does not consider evil. Yet in the animal kingdom this tendency is intrinsically evil. Just as the Fall involves humans falling back into animality, so a similar satanic corruption in the animal world involves slipping back into behavior proper to vegetables.[21] Animal pain is not God's handiwork but is begun by Satan's malice and perpetuated by Adam's desertion of his post. Lewis ventures the speculation that humans, at their first coming into the world, may already have had a redemptive function to perform, sharing in the rescue of creation from the corruption of Satan.[22] This thought could be suggested by the idea that humans were to have dominion, to subdue the earth in the sense that its disorder was to be overcome.

What is remarkable about this view is that, although it is coherent in its own terms, there is little that would specifically support it in Scripture. We have argued already that the fall of angels is only lightly represented, if at all, and there is nothing that may be held to shed light on the involvement of the power of darkness in the animal order. It might, however, be possible to argue that a process of deviation leading to suffering was already at work within nature prior to human beings. If nature has its own kind of freedom to explore its God-given potential by means of development and evolutionary processes, this opens up the possibility of wrong turns and wrong developments as part of this freedom. If creation itself is pressured by the possibility of collapse back into the chaos then this could have an effect on creation.[23] N. P. Williams developed at this point the idea of an "aberration in the life force."[24] Human beings are then born into this pre-existing condition and their own kind of fall is precipitated.

Physical evil and the shadow across creation. A fourth response to the question of physical evil is that the majority of what is called "physical evil" is misnamed, and creation as it is, apart from the moral evil of free creatures, is substantially, although not entirely, as God intended it. This approach does not accept that creation was precipitated into a fallen state but that the creation was, from the beginning, acquainted with the kinds of conflicts we are here discussing.

To develop this point of view we return to the concept of the "Shadow" of which Carl Jung speaks. This concept as expounded by Jung led to the enthronement of Satan as a member of the Godhead. This we rejected as a fatal mistake. Yet the thought that there is a shadow side to creation has been advanced by Karl Barth in a way that avoids this by distinguishing radically between "the Shadow" and "Nothingness," that is to say, evil. By the Shadow,[25] Barth means that creation and existence involve both negative and positive aspects. The negative aspects are not to be identified as evil but seen as parts of God's good creation. The

Shadow includes "hours, days and years both bright and dark, success and failure, laughter and tears, growth and age, gain and loss, birth and sooner or later its inevitable corollary, death."[26] He here indicates that creation has its threatening side, and this is not in itself evil.

Humankind was not placed into a world where it would be cushioned from discomfort, struggle and effort, failure or disappointment, but into a world where they would undergo a soul-making experience, which would cause them to grow to maturity through the struggle, difficulty and demand of earthly existence. The Shadow exists in creation not as something evil in itself but as that which would cause humankind to depend on God for help and strength. This Shadow does not jeopardize the nature of the creation as "very good" since God's judgment in Genesis 1:31 does not imply that the creation was perfect and without negative aspects. Rather, the goodness of creation consists in its being suitable for God's purposes and for humankind within them.[27] It is an appropriate sphere for people to learn relationship with God. According to Barth, creaturely being contains two aspects, a Yes and a No, joy and misery, but both have their foundation in the will of God and are reflections of the majesty and lowliness of God himself.[28]

It may appear that Barth is saying what we have already rejected, namely that evil is really good. The crucial point is his clear distinction between the Shadow and Nothingness. The Shadow belongs to that category of events and experiences that are at the time difficult, but for which we are grateful in due course because we recognize that we have benefited through them. Evil, on the other hand, is not of this character. It is utterly evil and is not created by God. The point is that *evil uses the Shadow as an alibi.*[29] It hides behind it and persuades people that it is identical with it. The result is that we run two dangers. On the one hand, we may call evil good because we confuse it with the Shadow (as did Jung). On the other hand, for the same reason we may end up calling the Shadow evil. We need to distinguish between the two quite clearly.

There are difficult experiences in life that belong to the Shadow yet serve us by enabling us to become more fully human. In the list mentioned above, Barth even includes death in these experiences, not meaning death as we now experience it in our fallen state (that is death in alienation) but rather the cessation of earthly existence that we would have experienced in fellowship with God had we not fallen, which contains its own challenges nonetheless. Through these experiences of being on the boundary we actually experience growth to maturity and should therefore confess them as good. But evil is that power at work in the world about which nothing good should be said or thought. For this irrational, absurd and destructive power human beings should entertain nothing but scorn.

How does this concept help us in understanding physical evil? It asserts that there is a Shadow in creation that consists in decay, death and conflict. Properly described, this Shadow would not be called evil. It is dark, but it is not evil because it is created by God and provides the kind of environment in which humankind may learn to depend on God. The natural world as we know it is substantially as God made it. Indeed, there is a logic to its apparent conflicts. Martin Israel, writing both as a priest and as a pathologist with a keen sense for the workings of evolution and the natural order, writes:

> It often strikes me how even ferocious animals and poisonous snakes have an important role to play in modifying our ecological environment. This they do in destroying such living creatures as feed on their own environment without any restraint, and left to their own devices would rapidly procreate without any restraint until the world was overcrowded and widespread famine the inevitable outcome.[30]

He draws from this a conclusion that runs counter to the argument we are pursuing:

> I personally feel that what we call "evil" is part of the divine creation, al-

most the divine will, for without the constant challenge to grow in spiritual awareness and stature, by which I mean becoming less self-centred and more dedicated to the welfare of all our fellow creatures (the vegetable and animal groups as well as the human one), the more we would remain stuck in an all too easy complacency. . . . I see that it plays a paradoxical part in the divine economy.[31]

By contrast Barth's view distinguishes between the Shadow and evil in such a way as to find place for aspects of the natural order that are fierce and indeed troubling. But into this world has come an alien power, which is genuinely evil. From our present vantage point it may be difficult to disentangle evil from the Shadow and so what belongs to either will only finally be disclosed at the end, when God's purposes are fulfilled. What we do know is that the time is coming when the creation itself will lose its shadow side of decay and death and enter into liberty, but it will only do so in fellowship with the children of God at the consummation of all things (Rom 8:18-21). And if the "theological poetics" of Jürgen Moltmann are to be believed, that day may also mean a healing of the sufferings and ravages of an evolutionary creation, as the process of creation is itself redeemed through Christ by a dynamic reaching back out of the future into time:

> It is the divine tempest of the new creation, which sweeps out of God's future over history's fields of the dead, waking and gathering every last created being. The raising of the dead, the gathering of the victims and the seeking of the lost bring a redemption of the world which no evolution can ever achieve.[32]

The conclusion of this discussion is that not all "pain" is evil, but evil uses pain as an alibi and disguises itself behind it. Some pain is evil—the kind that is meaningless, irrational and essentially cruel, with no soul-making purpose in view. A great deal of pain that is experienced in and inflicted by the human race can be seen to fit into this evil category. This approach to the problem of physical evil enables us to affirm the soul-making value of humankind's facing a creation that is, in some respects, threatening and dark yet essentially good. It also enables us to recognize evil for what it is and to reject it.

The fall into moral evil has introduced its own kind of distortion and disruption into the creation as human beings have achieved greater and greater capacity to exploit and spoil the environment.

This approach avoids the need to explain away the presence of decay and death in the creation before the Fall of Adam. It also avoids the contortionism of some varieties of scientific creationism and fits more easily into the description of the world and its development that is given in modern scientific research.

Have we then given a sufficient answer to the problem of evil? Despite all the discussion of this chapter the answer must be no. There is no straightforward answer. It may be that we can give an intellectual response that shows how Christians may consistently and honestly believe in a God who is both almighty and all loving. The free will defense enables this to happen. But beyond the arguments there is the fact of meaningless and mindless evil, which needs a different kind of answer than religious philosophy can give. The kind of suffering faced by Eli Wiesel and millions of others cannot be understood easily. This is the point where words reach their useful limit. Of course, the very irrationality and absurdity of evil means that we will always struggle to comprehend it. The difficulty in explaining it has more than a little to do with its essential nature as that which defies reason and explanation and flies in the face of sense and meaning.

Beyond this we point to the fact that the God who is revealed in Jesus and who has created us is not removed from human suffering. The idea that God is an impassable Being who is untouched by our pain is an inadequate one. The God revealed in the cross of Jesus has embraced our human suffering yet possesses the resources to overcome and not fall prey to it. He knows what it is to be rejected and to suffer. We can assert that God is with us even when, perhaps most especially when, we experience pain and sorrow and do not understand why. Eli Wiesel goes on in his book to record a most horrific incident in the death camp where he experienced hell on earth. He describes how two men and a child were hanged before the camp. The two men were defiant in death, but the child remained silent. As they were made to watch the scene, one of the camp inmates cried out "Where is God? Where is he now?" The men were to die quickly, but because he was so light, the child did not die so easily.

> For more than half an hour he stayed there, struggling between life and earth, dying in slow agony under our eyes. And we had to look him full in the face. He was still alive when I passed in front of him. His tongue was still red, his eyes were not yet glazed. Behind me, I heard the same man asking "Where is God now?" And I heard a voice within me answer him: "Where is He? Here He is—He is hanging here on this gallows."[33]

It belongs to the mystery of the book whether Wiesel means that God also has died or whether in some profoundly mysterious way the God who knows about suffering is with those who suffer. God is the God of the cross, the crucified God who has suffered with and for us in order that he may be the Father of those who suffer. What Christians can offer in the face of suffering is not a philosophical answer to humankind's vulnerability. Rather it is faith in the God of the cross and resurrection, who alone has conquered evil and is able to make it, against its own nature, serve the good of his creatures.

CHAPTER SIX

INSIDE INFORMATION?

We have been working to gain a perspective on the power of darkness that will help us to see it for what it is, neither exaggerating and exalting its power, nor minimizing and disregarding it. We have sought to unmask the nature of evil and the form it takes in our world. On this basis, it is now our intention to examine the activity of evil and to suggest ways in which, through the crucified, risen and exalted Christ, its work may be undone.

At this point in our inquiry, we reflect on the progress of charismatic renewal. It is largely in charismatic circles that the awareness of the demonic has come into new prominence. This is not surprising. First, the charismatic movement is essentially concerned with the renewal of the Spirit's power in the church. It bears testimony to a quickening of God's power in the experience of Christians and in mission to the world. If this claim is true, the renewal of spiritual power should lead to conflict with opposing powers in the world. Second, the renewing work of the Spirit brings with it a renewal of his gifts, such as those described in 1 Corinthians 12:7-11. Listed here is "the ability to distinguish between spirits" (v. 10). Arnold Bittlinger understands this as the "ability to distinguish between divine, human and demonic powers" and sees this gift manifested in the encounter of Peter with Simon Magus (Acts 8:20-24) and his exposure of Ananias and Sapphira (Acts 5:3). Paul exhibits the gift in his recognition that Bar-Jesus is a son of the devil (Acts 13:10) and in perceiving that the slave girl in Philippi was controlled by a spirit of divination (Acts 16:17-18).[1] If this gift is being rekindled in the church, it should be no surprise if it occasionally turns up results.

It is largely through charismatic renewal that the awareness of demonic powers has been stimulated in the church, and it was early in the movement that the theme began to come into prominence.[2] Many Christians had already been prepared for this emphasis in the popular writings of C. S. Lewis, who expressed the theme in both his fiction and apologetics. In more recent years the theme of spiritual warfare has broadened out. The concern for many charismatic groups has become corporate spiritual warfare operating with the belief that there are powers of darkness that can control and dominate society. These powers are known as "territorial spirits" and are engaged and confronted by means of "strategic-level spiritual warfare," through words of authority that throw back their influence and reclaim the territory for God.[3] This philosophy lay behind the "Make Way" marches that were designed to proclaim the lordship of Christ in localities, thereby reinforcing the dethroning of the dark powers that afflict society. This view of spiritual warfare will be the subject of a later chapter. It indicates that the conception of spiritual warfare in charismatic circles is in development.

This chapter examines demonic interference in the lives of individuals, usually called "demon possession," "oppression" or "infestation," the solution to which is known as "deliverance" or "exorcism." More recently reference has been to "demonization" as this is more biblically accurate[4] and more suitable pastorally in that it indicates the imprecise nature of much demonic interference. The method we follow will be to examine four differing accounts of the phenomenon of demonization, and its remedy in deliverance ministry, before going on to analyze what is being claimed.

FOUR ACCOUNTS OF DEMONIZATION

The Blumhardt experience. We begin with an experience that is not well known yet has exercised a profound influence in the German-speaking world. This is the remarkable story of a Lutheran pastor called Johann Christoph Blumhardt (1805-1880) who ministered at a village called Möttlingen from 1838-1852. Blumhardt belonged to the pietist wing of the Lutheran church that emphasized the need for experience of God, but was not typical of this tradition, as he preserved a strong emphasis on the objective work of Christ and a universal hope for the world. While in Möttlingen he unexpectedly experienced a very dramatic encounter with demonic forces afflicting a parishioner named Gottliebin Dittus. He later described his two-year struggle to rescue this woman in a report to his local synod.[5] In measured and sober terms he describes how Gottliebin, a devout and otherwise unremarkable woman of twenty-eight, suffered from various physical ailments and began from 1840 to experience strange phenomena in her apartment along with disturbing physical interference. The phenomena included the appearance of figures, noises in the house and the materialization of objects. When prayed for, she would experience convulsions. Blumhardt became convinced that these were demonic in origin, and after declaring "we have seen long enough what the devil is doing, now we also want to see what Jesus can do," things took a major turn for the better.[6] The pattern of convulsion and prayer leading to deliverance continued for some time, accompanied by the most bizarre and horrific phenomena. Demons spoke out of her claiming to be the spirits of deceased people and angels of Satan.[7] Gottliebin's sister, Katharina, and her brother showed symptoms of similar demonization until the final moment of deliverance came on December 28, 1843. The battle centered, at this point, around Katharina. Blumhardt writes:

> Finally the most moving moment came which no-one can possibly imagine who was not an eye and ear witness. At two o'clock in the morning the supposed angel of Satan roared, while the girl bent back her head and upper part of her body over the backrest of the chair, with a voice of

which one would hardly have believed a human throat capable, "Jesus is Victor! Jesus is Victor!"—words that sounded so far and were understood at such a distance that they made an unforgettable impression on many people. Now the power and strength of the demon seemed to be broken more with every moment. It became ever more quiet and calmer, could only make a few motions and finally disappeared unnoticed like the life-light of a dying person goes out.[8]

The outcome of the conflict was that the family was restored to a peaceful and healthful state. Gottliebin recovered from all her former illnesses to develop as a deeply spiritual person with a loving and kind ministry as a schoolteacher.[9] The impact of the incident was such as to spark off a wave of spiritual renewal. Blumhardt became a popular preacher and, between 1852 and 1880, was the leader of a renewal center at Bad Boll, which played the same kind of role in Germany that Keswick played in England. The characteristic theme of the renewal movement was the phrase "Jesus is Victor!"—a phrase later picked up and extensively used by the theologian Karl Barth, prompting the comment "the voice of the devil is an unexpected source for modern theology!"[10]

Most remarkable is to trace the effect of Blumhardt and his son Christoph Friedrich on twentieth-century theology. Barth was influenced by them at the time of his own theological revolution during the First World War.[11] Emil Brunner, Oscar Cullmann and Dietrich Bonhoeffer are all theologians who acknowledge a debt to the Blumhardt inheritance.[12] All of this would indicate that the "murky performances at Möttlingen"[13] should not be too easily dismissed as the superstitious and naive interpretations of an unsophisticated country parson. Blumhardt was sober, intelligent, educated, accurate and highly respected. Nothing in the circumstances of his life or in the spirit of the age would have predisposed him to find demons in his parishioner. For him it was unexpected and unlooked for.

Although I trembled through every paragraph, thinking whether it might not be hasty and careless to tell everything so clearly, I felt the urge within me again and again, "Tell it all."[14]

War on the saints. In 1904 the Welsh Revival led to the conversion of large numbers and had an enduring impact on the social life of the people. An estimated one hundred thousand were converted. One of the chief human instruments in the revival was Evan Roberts who paid such a physical price that his health was broken. He lived the life of a semi-invalid until his death in 1951.[15] Another major figure was Jessie Penn-Lewis, who wrote a book in collaboration with Roberts, titled *War on the Saints*, detailing experiences in the wake of the revival.[16] The book is a highly detailed description of the deceptive workings of the powers of darkness. It claims that demons are at work in abundance, deceiving and possessing individuals, including Christians.[17] Indeed a danger point is when a Christian is baptized in the Holy Spirit, since at this point of abandonment to the invisible and supernatural he or she becomes vulnerable to deception.[18] Evil spirits, either prior to or after this time, gain access to the body or mind and hide deeply in the structure of the person, becoming to all intents and purposes part of him or her. It is the lack of discernment and ignorance of Christians that renders them so vulnerable.[19]

War on the Saints is a disturbing book. It came out of the spiritual turbulence that occurred in the aftermath of the revival. As in previous times of revival it became clear that not all the phenomena that accompanied it were unproblematic. There were counterfeits. There was a mixture of good and bad in the experience of those who had been visited. Many of the phenomena initially considered signs of the presence of God were felt in time to be spurious. These observations need to be reflected on.

But the book is disturbing for another reason, namely the picture it draws of the almost complete vulnerability of ordinary Christians to demonic attack. If the danger of deception is so great, it is only the mature and discerning (and perhaps not even they?) who are in a position to withstand. We are left with a rather hopeless picture of a church in which the ordinary person is acted on by evil powers in a highly exposed way. After all, if to be baptized in the Holy Spirit renders one vulnerable to invisible and supernatural invasion by the enemy, what hope is there for any of us? Where is the comfort given by Jesus to the effect that "nothing will harm you" (Lk 10:19)?

Here we begin to see the need for the groundwork developed in the earlier parts of this book. Whatever insights are contained in Jessie Penn-Lewis's book, there is such a concentration on the demonic and such a ready acceptance of the power of the enemy that this way of thinking serves to increase the power of what is otherwise so energetically resisted. The world becomes the province of demons. A "demon consciousness" is encouraged, which gives them the attention and respect they thrive and trade on. In preference to this we need to assume the position of scorn and of radical disbelief in relation to the demonic.

Pigs in the Parlor. In 1973 Frank and Ida Mae Hammond published *Pigs in the Parlor*, describing their experience of deliverance ministry and of giving practical guidance in this area.[20] At that time Frank Hammond had enjoyed twenty-five years as a Baptist pastor, held two degrees and had only recently entered into the deliverance realm. The title of the book draws a parallel between the unclean swine of the Old Testament and evil spirits in the New. The need for deliverance is, in their opinion, very widespread. Indeed, Frank writes: "Does everyone need deliverance? Personally, I have not found any exceptions."[21]

Satan's kingdom is an organized one. It involves a "prince spirit" set over each local church that accounts for the specific types of problems faced by it on a recurring basis. Examples of these include "doctrinal demons," or demons of false doctrine (1 Tim 4:1). Likewise, nations and communities have "ruling demon potentates," along the lines of the "prince of Persia" against which Michael the archangel fought (Dan 10:13). Demons operate in rough groupings, and it is common to find clusters of spirits of a similar type infesting an individual.[22] Certain combinations of spirits can be found working together, for instance, to produce schizophrenia.[23] When this is understood by the deliverance minister it becomes possible to root out the spirits that afflict in this way. Deliverance is generally assisted by being able to identify a spirit by name and command it specifically to leave. This may be done by the one who ministers, by oneself or even by proxy for another.[24] According to the book, when deliverance is engaged in, the exit of the demon takes place through the mouth or nose and may be indicated by the expulsion of breath or by coughing.[25] Even children need deliverance, but this normally is more easily achieved.[26]

The Hammonds offer us a world in which demons are highly active and where many ailments, physical or mental, have their roots in demonization. Their mapping of the demonic kingdom has been discovered by the actual experience of ministering deliverance. This raises the question of how much credibility can be given to the experience of individuals when there is little or no biblical warrant for the kinds of detailed descriptions they go in for. Generally, the book demonstrates a very literal approach to Scripture, as perceived in the strange remarks about the sinister nature of owls and frogs. Concern is expressed that these creatures, described in Deuteronomy 14:7-19 as unclean and regarded as "types" of evil spirits, are being made into art objects and decorations. That they are animals of the night also counts against them.[27] One wonders what doctrine of creation lies behind this thinking. There is a form of biblical naiveté at work here that does not evidence much theological acumen.

Demons Defeated. A further book to have enjoyed wide popularity was written by New Zealand lawyer and Anglican layperson Bill Subritzky. Like the Hammonds he describes his own discovery of the deliverance ministry, in his case through his son's deliverance.[28] Approaching Scripture in an unsophisticated and highly subjective way, he describes how "Satan places unseen princes and powers of the air over every nation and city with descending orders of authority all the way down to demons which walk on the ground and seek a home."[29] There are three primary "strong men," or spiritual forces, which Subritzky names as the spirits of Jezebel, Antichrist, and Death and Hell. Together these are the satanic counterparts of the Holy Trinity.[30] Under the direction of these strongmen, demons are highly active in the world and can enter people in many ways, including through heredity, parental rejection, contact with demonized people, curses and rock music.[31] When ministering deliverance it is helpful, according to Subritzky, to know that there is a "leader of the pack" among the demons. Frequently this is one of the strongmen mentioned above. Other demons, some of them with identical names, will cluster around this leader.[32] In the deliverance process, the presence of angels is an occasional experience.[33] Once delivered it is essential to live a sanctified life in order to keep the deliverance received.[34]

The purpose of reviewing these books has not been to give an exhaustive analysis of them but to indicate their adopted way of thinking. The last three books in particular have exercised a wide, popular influence and are referred to by many as formative of their thinking in this area.[35] They indicate particular (and idiosyncratic) points of view, both in the interpretation and application of Scripture. Other books could be referred to on the popular level,[36] and some of a more substantial nature,[37] which cover the same ground, albeit with variations. However, these approaches raise immense questions. If what they describe is true, then a radical readjustment is necessary in our way of looking at the world and in our method of ministry within it. If, on the other hand, it is mistaken, we are being led into areas of superstition and delusion that will not profit us. What are we to make of it all? We proceed by examining some objections to the whole approach and attempting to make our way through the minefield. The conclusion we shall reach is that demonization is a reality and we need to know how to deal with it. However, much that is written in these books is fantasy, and we need to take great care that it does not get out of hand.

DEALING WITH THE DIFFICULTIES

No return to the Dark Ages. One straightforward response to the above accounts of demonization and deliverance is to reject it as nonsense perpetrated by credulous and deluded individuals. A world populated by demons in the ways described is rejected as primitive, pre-scientific and pre-Enlightenment, not to be entertained by thinking people in the twentieth century. What is needed is not deliverance from evil spirits but deliverance from belief in them. When this whole area was discussed in the mid-1970s, Professor Geoffrey Lampe and Don Cupitt produced an open letter signed by sixty-five theologians, which asserted:

> It is, we think, mistaken to suppose that loyalty to Christ requires the Church to recreate, in late twentieth century Europe, the outlook and practices of first century Palestine. Such an attempt invites ridicule, not to mention the harm that may be done. We urge all who hold high office in the Church to ensure that the practice of exorcism receives no official encouragement and gains no official status in the Church.[38]

Belief in spirits is not binding on Christians today simply because Jesus believed in them any more than it is mandatory for Christians to wear sandals, robes and long hair. In the ancient world everybody believed in spirits and today nobody with any grasp of the modern worldview does. However, both these points of view are suspect. First, not everybody in the ancient world believed in the existence of demons, and therefore the fact that Jesus did is significant. Second, there is much evidence to indicate that the scientific worldview does not adequately explain the total experience of humankind, and because of this, belief in dark powers is still a serviceable way of making sense of some aspects of actual experience. The first and twentieth centuries are not so different as might be supposed.[39] Accepting the reality of demons still remains a coherent way of describing reality.

This dogmatic approach must explain why those who speak of demons are not necessarily unenlightened, unintelligent or credulous people. Some of the literature produced creates this impression. But it is only part of a wider body of research in which educated and intelligent people from a broad spectrum of disciplines argue forcibly for the reality of this realm.[40] People experience phenomena of such intensity and such a type that they can be identified with those of the New Testament. The experiences are such that the only adequate explanation appears to be that of demonization. This impression is gained because of the clearly overpowering nature of what some individuals experience, because of the ability of the invading entity to speak through the voice of the individual concerned and because of a clear antipathy toward anything to do with Christ whether this be the mention of his name or of his work. The fact that other theories cannot explain these experiences, as well as the fact that ministry in the name of Jesus actually sets people free, has led large numbers of Christian ministers to revise their previously held skeptical views in this area.

Going beyond Scripture. A second objection is concerned that the Bible has little, other than incidentally, to say about demonology. This is a weighty objection. Whereas a central theme in the Bible is that Christ has come to destroy the work of the devil, the Bible is not interested in the kind of demonology that certain individuals have come to specialize in and be "authorities" on. There is something objectionable about investigating something the Bible considers not worth it. It is particularly disturbing when knowledge of the demonic "kingdom" is not derived from Christ but from demons themselves by the information they impart as to their own identity and activity. Is not this kind of inside information intrinsically wrong? And are not demons such inherently deceitful entities that distortion is bound to be present in anything derived from them? This matter is of such major importance that some cautionary assertions are essential.

- The New Testament shows no interest in demonology as such and only treats it as incidental to the positive work of Christ in bringing the kingdom of God. This is not to say that the expulsion of demons was a peripheral part of Christ's ministry. It clearly was both important and central, but it was one element of a total work of forgiveness, healing and liberation. In the church's ministry today we should expect it to be one, but only one, element of our work.

- The New Testament says very little about the internal workings of the kingdom of darkness. This leads to agnosticism concerning any particular account of how the demonic world ticks. Where truth is revealed in Scripture we can take an unequivocal stand on it. Where it is not, we must sit loose to anything that claims to "tell it as it is." The books that attempt to do this should not be taken as authoritative but as attempts to describe and make sense of experiences. They are bound to be defective to a greater or lesser degree.

  This is not to say that such experience is invalid simply because the Bible does not mention it. The Bible knows nothing, for instance, of the post-Freudian account of the working of the human personality, yet it is taken for granted today that the kind of knowledge gained through psychology and psychiatry is essential for wise pastoral care. Knowledge of which the Bible does not specifically speak may be gained in the practice of the Christian life. There is an analogy here with the counseling disciplines. The proponents of the various schools of counseling tend to think that they each have the right approach. In reality each account offers a model that is at best an imprecise way of understanding the workings of the human soul. We should take the same attitude toward the various descriptions of deliverance. Nobody has the ultimate viewpoint. Some may have gotten it completely wrong.

- It is surely mistaken to conceive of the demonic realm as well organized and highly structured. Its essence is not reason but unreason, not organization but chaos. "The inconsistent, incoherent and chaotic nature of evil besets an enquiry into the existence of demons so that one's results will have to remain tentative."[41] Given this we should expect that demonic activity changes from place to place, from age to age and from moment to moment. Accounts that outline the shape of the demonic organization are to be treated with extreme skepticism.

- This last point is followed by one of the same kind. We need to beware of the danger of finding what we expect to find. All counselors will be aware of the danger of imposing their own expectations and models on their counselees. It is a matter of human fact that, given the kind of reciprocal relationship that makes counseling possible, counselees will knowingly or unknowingly come up with what their counselors are felt to be looking for. If we have too clear a notion of what we are looking for in the demonic realm it comes as no surprise that we keep on finding it. There are intricate and subtle interpersonal factors at work here.

These cautionary words help us hold fast to Scripture and sit loose to everything else. At the same time it is possible to exaggerate the silence of Scripture in this field. Encounter with the demonic often leads to renewed reflection on the details of the biblical accounts. It can be deduced that demonization might involve large numbers of demonic entities (for example "Legion"); that they produce symptoms of madness and distress as well as physical illness; that there are different kinds of demons and that some are particularly difficult to get rid of (Mt 17:21); that they are capable of speaking through individuals; and that they can produce extraordinary violence in those they infest (Acts 19:14-16). Nevertheless, all of these details are incidental, and the balance of the New Testament is worthy of imitation. Whereas it accepts the reality of the demonic, it never shows more than a passing interest in it. In the light of this it is to be seriously questioned whether it is spiritually profitable to publish books, produce tapes or run courses in this area, other than those that are of the most restrained kind. The effect of these is all too often to create an unhealthy demon mentality in overreceptive minds.

The paranoid worldview. This brings us to a third objection. If the world really is so highly infested with demons as some suggest, what are the implications of this for the way we look at the world? Is not attributing so much activity to the demons imminently in danger of pandering to the paranoia, the mental delusion of persecution and conspiracy, which is characteristic of the neurotic personality and which lurks not far beneath the surface of most of us? The force of this criticism is considerable, particularly in the light of pastoral experience that indicates there are those who see demons everywhere. If the vocabulary and thought forms Christians use stimulate this morbid neurosis we need to pay attention to both.

For the moment our concern is firmly with demonization in its individual expression and with counteracting "demonmania," the overinclination to explain things in terms of the demonic. One way we can do this is to ask, how frequent is demonization? According to Frank Hammond, everybody in his experience is demonized to some degree. Subritzky and Penn-Lewis would see it as very widespread. There seems little concept of wider factors in the spiritual, mental and social health of those concerned. Demons have become the grid through which personal problems are viewed, and deliverance ministers have become one-club golfers who only have one iron with which to play.

Others who accept the reality of demonization nevertheless see it as a rare occurrence. In the report of the Christian Exorcism Study Group, which can scarcely be described as unspiritually skeptical, possession by an evil spirit is held to take place only when the individual puts him or herself in a vulnerable position and deliberately invites invasion. It may also occur through indirect contact with blatant forms of the occult.[42] A previous report on exorcism edited by Dom Robert Petitpierre also sees possession as very rare, although real.[43] A psychiatrist with wide experience in this field put the number of his patients needing exorcism at around four percent.[44] Another psychiatrist is quite skeptical, finding the many cases cited by Kurt Koch, for instance, "very unconvincing."[45]

Part of this wide discrepancy among those who are disposed to accept the possibility of demonic interference may be explained by different ways of understanding "possession." For some, it is the extreme point of a spectrum of demonic onslaught ranging from temptation through obsession and oppression to possession.[46] It is therefore rare. Others reject possession language and speak of demonization as referring to forms of demonic penetration to a greater or lesser degree. The equation requires that wherever there is some penetration of sin (that is everywhere) there will be some demonic interference.[47] A Christian therefore could never be "demon possessed" since this would imply ownership by demons, but he or she could be trespassed on unlawfully by demons.[48] This takes us into areas we have yet to discuss. There is disagreement over the degree to which demons are active in the world. Some see them as a sinister element in a total picture of human fallenness. Others see them as the primary agents of all forms of human sin and affliction. The former of these attitudes is surely by far the healthier to entertain. It does not lead to demonmania but takes more seriously the role of human responsibility. It avoids giving demons a glory and power that is not theirs. That demons are as active as some suppose is a simplistic approach that does not take seriously enough the other dimensions of human nature and sin. This brings us to a further objection in this area.

Can't "demonization" be adequately explained in other ways? Here is a major question. Granted that those who deal with demons are experiencing something that looks like demonization, have they the right interpretation of the phenomena? Do they have it in every case? Could it not be explained quite adequately by reference to psychological factors? If so it becomes dangerous and pastorally irresponsible in the extreme to suggest to people (who may be very open to suggestion) that they have a demon problem. A Christian psychiatrist, Dr. Monty Barker, draws attention to a group of twenty disturbed people for whom he was clinically responsible, whose average age was twenty-two, with high intelligence and mainly Christian backgrounds. "A high proportion had been in contact with charismatic groups. A number had had the idea suggested to them that they were possessed. Some had received exorcism, one on three occasions." His conclusion was that none of them were demonized, but those who felt themselves to be so were externalizing their own conflicts and distresses as demons. In this way "the search for solutions can be given up and responsibility handed over to the demons and to the exorcist."[49]

It is plain that we are in a complex realm. This should warn us against simplistic explanations. To gain perspective I venture some tentative reflections drawn from experience.

HUMAN BEINGS ARE PSYCHOLOGICALLY MORE COMPLEX THAN WE IMAGINE

Put briefly, individuals can manifest all the symptoms of demonization when in reality their difficulties are psychological in origin. To treat them as if they are demonized is both to confirm their false perception of the situation and to collude with them in it. It is a pastoral error invasive of personality. The strange forms of behavior that lead the unskilled person to assume demonic activity may indicate nothing more than a disordered inner life with complex psychological origins. The power of the unconscious in humans is immense. Out of it can come the most surprising things, including reactions that may on the face of it look demonic. In reality they may be repressed emotions, buried hurts, unacknowledged frustrations or complex elements of personality that have been denied, split off and made into autonomous elements of the person's inner being.[50] The same symptoms may be produced by different causes. Some people enjoy the intense attention given to those afflicted by demons, so they produce the symptoms for as long as it keeps them in the limelight. Others absorb the time and energy of Christian people to divert them from other tasks. Critics draw attention to the way in which so many Christians find themselves to have demons and suggest that this may be because they have been brought up in an oppressive religion that has caused them to "split off" what others manage to integrate.[51]

HUMAN BEINGS ARE SOCIALLY MORE COMPLEX THAN WE IMAGINE

I open up two possibilities. The first is suggestibility. In the dependent and trusting relationships that develop between individuals in need and their counselors there can enter in a form of illusion. The counselee responds to the suggestions of the counselor and produces the responses felt to be expected. Sometimes these are suddenly discovered as repressed memories. Thereby he or she confirms the expectations of the counselor, and the cycle goes on. It is not uncommon in the sphere of deliverance to observe a bonding between counselor and counselee in which there is a merging of conceptual horizons, a sense of solidarity against the rest of the world and a loss of the critical objectivity that enables a retreat from a misdiagnosis toward a more adequate diagnosis. The counselee wishes to avoid questioning the counselor, and the counselor cannot face the possible disappointment of the counselee. Neither dare appear "unspiritual" by suggesting a natural rather than supernatural cause for the presenting symptoms. When this dynamic is compounded by the involvement of others who are convinced about the demonic cause, a situation has been produced from which it is difficult to extricate oneself.

The second possibility is that individuals become the victims of a group mentality that is demon-minded and imprisons them within this thought form. If the dominant ethos of a group, church or otherwise, is inclined to find demons at work and perceives a group member's problem to be along these lines, the group pressure may prove too difficult to resist. The victim is faced with the choice of forsaking the group, with all the emotional difficulties that would entail, or of obediently playing along and producing the appropriate forms of behavior. It must be stressed that this process operates primarily on the subconscious level and people may be totally unconscious of what is happening. It is not surprising if the individual is carried along by the group for some time before finding the burden intolerable and opting out.

HUMAN BEINGS ARE PSYCHICALLY MORE COMPLEX THAN WE IMAGINE

It is a feature of revivals and powerful spiritual visitations that in the wake of a genuine movement of the Spirit there are spurious phenomena. Jonathan Edwards wrote a major treatise on this subject after the eighteenth-century revival in New England when some of the post-revival phenomena threatened to bring the revival into question as a genuine work of God.[52] Precisely the same problem was experienced after the Welsh Revival of 1904, which was strongly marked by spiritual ferment and physical manifestations of the presence of God's Spirit, and in more recent movements such as the Third Wave and the "Toronto Blessing."[53] It is not my intention to cast doubt on the validity of such happenings but to draw attention to the aftermath in which phenomena can continue, as it were, under their own steam. Martyn Lloyd-Jones, a keen student and advocate of revival, described this possibility as "the danger of passing from the spiritual to the psychological and even the psychic."[54]

In all spiritual affairs we need to be aware that phenomena that exceed the conscious capacity and ability of individuals may have their origin not in the Spirit of God, nor necessarily in evil spirits, but simply in forms of psychic energy that are deeper even than the subconscious mind. In saying this I am aware that scientific definitions of the human psyche do not have much place for what I am calling the *psychic*. It appears necessary however to speak of such a dimension to explain my own pastoral experience and that of others.

It is significant that the report of the Christian Exorcism Study Group takes this energy source with considerable seriousness and finds it possible to explain much paranormal activity (but not all) without reference to the demonic. It has its origin in the psychic reservoirs that some people develop the ability to tap. Manipulations of the psychic were forbidden in Scripture "because they involved a divided loyalty to the Lord, and therefore hampered people from developing along the lines God willed."[55] The realm of the psychic may be regarded as neither holy nor demonic in itself but when oriented toward God it becomes integrated with the total life in communion with God. When oriented toward the devil it becomes the realm of unwholesome demonic activity. When not surrendered to God, and even if not consciously surrendered to darkness, it remains capable of being invaded to greater or lesser degrees depending on the residual character and will of the individual. For this reason, to develop this area independently of God is fraught with dangers. Even for the Christian the realm of the psychic should not be developed independently or self-consciously but should simply take its place in the yielding of the total person to God's Spirit, thus finding its true integration in the total person and especially in unity with the mind and in the Spirit of God.

The point of this extended (but important) discussion is to indicate that the inner life of people is also complex. For this reason we are told to test the spirits. Not all unusual and apparently "spiritual" phenomena are properly of God. They may be psychic. Conversely, not all apparently sinister "spiritual" occurrences are demonic. They also may be psychic in nature. From this several conclusions are to be drawn.

- First, there is the possibility that phenomena, which are taken in deliverance ministry to be demons, are in fact to be understood as elements of "psychic turbulence" that will react to exorcism but for which exorcism is inappropriate. In a deliverance situation, words of authority spoken by respected authority figures and addressed to the subconscious may well produce an effect and cause a reaction. It may be that such words will confront an area of sinfulness or hurt or long-repressed and forgotten memories and produce a result that resembles a demonic deliverance. Yet to see it as such is to misunderstand it.

- Second, given such a situation of deliverance ministry, an individual is without knowing it pushed into areas of imagination where they fantasize events and incidents that have a certain coherence but really come under the category of a false memory syndrome. Imaginations are fed by what has been seen, heard and read over many years, as well as by that of which the imagination functioning on the boundary is naturally capable. While receiving ministry, a counselee may supply the counselor with plausible but unreal stories of demonic intrigue, which at the time are believed to be true.

  As reported in chapter one, in the 1980s a rash of stories of satanic ritual abuse began to emerge. In a climate in which people were being encouraged to believe tales of abuse, the stories were widely accepted in Christian and social work circles. In the light of the government report that in time dismissed the whole frenzy as without substance, the onus is on those who believe in the factuality of satanic ritual abuse to prove their case. Otherwise it ought to be regarded as on par with those thousands of people who are unshakably persuaded that they have been abducted by aliens.[56]

  On two occasions individuals whom I have counseled have told me of their recovered memories of satanic conspiracies. There was a similarity to them and, indeed, to reports over the years about child murders (some of which have been laid at the doors of the Christian church), that suggests to me there is a buried archetype in the unconscious mind that reverts to this fantasy.

- Third, the situation is to be imagined where an individual is actually demonized and receives liberating ministry. But having under demonic influence reacted in certain ways to the ministry received (shaking, coughing, groaning and the like), he or she continues to respond to further prayer and ministry in this way not because he or she is still demonized but because he or she has entered subconsciously or psychically into autonomic responses to the personalities involved and to the words used in the counseling situation. Where this is the case, exorcism is no longer appropriate and needs to be replaced by a form of therapy that will help the individual to return to an ordered and peaceful existence.

HUMAN BEINGS ARE SPIRITUALLY MORE COMPLEX THAN WE IMAGINE

We have already touched on the complexity of human beings in the previous section. The intention here is to underline it by arguing that, in addition to the devil, Christians war against the flesh. The *flesh* can account for many of the phenomena that are described by the incautious as demonic. To illustrate this we refer to the ambiguity of the word *spirit*. This can describe an evil spirit or an attitude or an underlying disposition. We speak of a "spirit of pride" or a "spirit of gluttony" without at all intending a demonic entity but a sinful power with a foothold in an individual or a group. If so, deliverance or liberation from a concrete form of sin is needed. By virtue of its having become a binding power there may be a superficial resemblance here to a demon. Deliverance therefore should be seen as a spectrum extending at one end from the foothold that sin may have gained, through an ingrained habit or enslavement, through to actual and specific demonization. In a deliverance context, such binding sin might react to the name of Christ and might be mistaken for an evil spirit. My suspicion is that the majority of what is taken to be demonic in the books by Hammond and Subritzky is of this nature. Deliverance from binding sin is necessary, but this should not be administered under the form or under the name of exorcism. To do this is to take a hammer to crack a nut.

The object of this section has been to show that the area of deliverance is one of great complexity. This does not make it invalid. It may be that deliverance ministry is inappropriate and that many cases fit into the categories outlined above. It may be, however, that the symptoms that cause people to seek help actually do have as their cause some demonic affliction and that only this form of ministry will set them free. Perhaps few cases are clear cut and straightforward. People may be psychologically, socially, psychically and spiritually in need and, at the same time, be demonically afflicted. Cardinal Suenens once wrote:

> The fact that a phenomenon can be explained according to our scientific categories does not allow us to rule out the possibility of an interpretation belonging to another order or level of reality. We have to remind the scientist—if he is a Christian—that there are realities and dimensions which cannot be experimentally verified and that, furthermore, scientific objectivity does not allow us to dismiss other possible explanations in our interpretation of phenomena.[57]

We are justified in saying clearly that this complex area is not a place for the credulous and pastorally irresponsible. We should heed the warning of Kurt Koch that

> convinced occultists, spiritists and sadly, often simple and solid Christians also sometimes accept without question a belief in spirits and demons where this is completely unnecessary. Over and against this excessive belief in transcendent powers, we must seek the objective facts and sobriety and realism.[58]

Can Christians have demons? A fifth issue divides Christian opinion.

Deliverance ministry is practiced by Christians, and this is not surprising. It is also practiced on Christians, and this is surprising, or ought to be. How can Christians who are indwelt by the Holy Spirit be demonized? Furthermore, is there not a clash of authority at this point between those who base their case on the Bible, which does not appear to allow the possibility of demonized Christians, and those who appeal to the actual experience of encountering Christians who are demonized? If we appeal to experience, are we not left with subjective opinions?

It is plain that the Bible is the court of appeal for Christian believers. But what it says on specific pastoral issues is not always self-evident. Moreover, while experience is not the final authority for faith, experience does have to be made sense of. It raises questions and sheds light on the meaning of the biblical text. It is not enough to assert about any given experience that it contradicts the Bible. It may just contradict what we assume the Bible says. Therefore, we need to enter into the dialogue between experience and the biblical text. Concerning the relationship between Christians and evil spirits, we are able to assert the following.

- Everybody agrees that Christians can be tempted by the devil.

- Everybody agrees that Christians are prone to sin and have to struggle against the flesh, that is, the downward drag of those parts of our lives that remain unrenewed.

- Everybody agrees that Christians cannot be "possessed" by evil spirits since they belong to Christ.

  Some hold this to mean that no evil spirits can exist within a Christian since the Christian is the temple of the Holy Spirit and evil spirits could not peacefully coexist with the Holy Spirit. Those who consider Christians "demon proof" might consider it possible that under extreme circumstances they might be externally oppressed by spirits but not internally possessed.

  Others hold it to mean that while the spirit of the Christian, his or her innermost being, is indwelt by the Spirit, the outer regions of the person, that is the body and the outer areas of personality, can be infested. Yet a Christian cannot be possessed in an absolute sense.

Those who hold this view would not consider that such spirits could enter at will but would either be residual, leftover from the person's pre-Christian existence never having been expelled, or judgmental, having entered as a consequence of specific disobedience. When out of fellowship with God, individuals may make themselves vulnerable.

- What we consider the Bible to teach on this matter depends partly on which verses we select. So Luke 13:16 refers to a "daughter of Abraham" (which implies a devotion to God) who had been "kept bound" by Satan. In Mark 8:33 Jesus rebuked Peter with the words "Out of my sight, Satan." These might be held to imply a degree of access possible for the devil into the life of a believer on the basis of lack of sanctification. But these are not necessary interpretations. From another perspective, the words of Paul in 2 Corinthians 6:14-17—"What fellowship can light have with darkness? What harmony is there between Christ and Belial?"—points to the logical impossibility of such fellowship, not its actual impossibility when Christian living is inconsistent. As it happened, the impossible possibility of Christians being wrongfully associated and involved is precisely what was happening.

- The difficulties occur over this issue because of the spatial model of being indwelt by the Holy Spirit (1 Cor 3:16-17). Yet this is not the only model of Christian experience in the New Testament. Another is of Christians as battle zones where the Spirit of God and the sinful nature confront each other in hostility (Rom 8:5-8). This opens the possibility that the Spirit of God may on occasion not coexist with but confront an evil spirit on the frontier drawn across a human life.

- It becomes possible to conceive of demonic strongholds in the lives of individuals. If conversion is the process whereby God indwells individuals, this process is not completed immediately, otherwise Christians would not continue to sin. The reason demonic strongholds might continue to exist after regeneration is that we have reduced and devalued the conversion process. If an inadequate gospel is preached that does not bring about heartfelt repentance and does not stress the putting off of the old life, it is not surprising that darkness is not always rooted out as it should be.

In this context, it is worth noting that ancient and some modern baptismal practices make a place for clear and deliberate renunciation of the devil and all his works as part of the baptismal experience. Perhaps we need to return to this and to see the power of baptism in a new light.

- All these things said, enough has been explored earlier in this chapter to give a wide field to explore before it is necessary to conclude we are dealing with an evil spirit.

CONCLUSION

There is now available a body of literature that gives sound advice on how deliverance ministry, when it proves to be necessary, may be carried through in a way that is pastorally wise and sensitive. There is no need to repeat it here.[59] However, in the light of the cautionary words that have been written in this chapter it might prove helpful to highlight some points to supplement the literature that already exists.

- It is wise to be reluctant to conclude that a person is demonized. Therefore, every previous avenue normally needs to be explored before coming to this conclusion.

- Deliverance ministry should never be undertaken under pressure either from the individual concerned or from a group. It should only be attempted if there is a clear sense of direction and conviction from

God by people who know what they are doing.

- Wherever possible it is wise to have medical and psychiatric support in ministering to an individual. Some church disciplines require that permission is gained from a higher church authority before anything is done.

- Where it is possible to consult more experienced ministers, this should be done. Some church structures appoint consultants for this task.

- Deliverance should never be attempted alone. There should be at least two mature and experienced Christians present, and it is preferable that one should come from another church to provide objectivity. Obvious care needs to be taken when ministering to members of the opposite sex.

- Sessions of deliverance should not be protracted but should be for a set time and in a suitable context. It is important that those who minister should not find themselves being exhausted or their home life disrupted.

- Intense situations of mutual dependence should be avoided and a sense of critical distance maintained about the deliverance process.

- Each person should be treated with gentleness and respect at all times. There should be an avoidance of aggressive words, gestures or expressions, and a reliance on the authority of Christ.

- Demons should not be talked to, argued with or given any attention other than that of rejecting, refusing and scorning them.

- The use of holy water, crosses, sacred objects, communion wine or anointing oil in this context should be discouraged. It is the name of Christ alone that has power, and the use of physical means in a quasi-magical way heads in the wrong direction. It is not the minister who drives out demons but Christ. The name of Christ brings about the confrontation that will set people free.

- Deliverance should not be used for its sensation value in Christian testimony but should be discussed only when it is necessary and in discreet, sober and undramatic ways. It should not be gloried in (Lk 10:20) but seen as a necessary and routine task. It should be subject to the same ethics of confidentiality as any other form of counseling. It should take place within an accountability structure. Conversations that would elicit details for the wrong reasons should be refused.

- As in the ministry of Jesus the demonic factor and its remedy should not be given any more than incidental attention. "Demonmania" (seeing demons all over the place) is offensive to God and bad for the soul.

- Those who receive deliverance should be treated as individuals who bear responsibility for their own lives. It must be recognized that their freedom is dependent on their will to repent and be free. Deliverance is not a substitute for sturdy and responsible discipleship.

The object of all the remarks made in this chapter has been to encourage good attitudes and sensible practice. It is vital for the good of the renewing work taking place in the church that we get it right.

CHAPTER SEVEN

THE LORDLESS POWERS

The focus of the previous chapter was on the phenomenon of demonization evidenced in the lives of individuals. The church of Christ has much to offer those who are entangled and ensnared by demonic powers. We indicated the complexity of this issue and sounded cautious notes in light of the tendency, in some quarters, to heighten the matter, which trivializes the issue and makes it all the easier to reject. For example, when taken to extremes, it can be argued that belief in demons is a distinctly unhealthy thing, a symptom of neurotic religion growing out of an insidious paranoia. It can be claimed that the very idea of demons is unhelpful in that it encourages people to avoid responsibility for their own behavior, giving them opportunity to blame their sins on an external cause.

The force of all these criticisms needs to be felt. All of them are true of certain people at certain times. None of this necessarily invalidates the idea that demonic entities are real any more than paranoid and neurotic attitudes to Soviet Russia in the days of the Cold War could be held to prove that the Kremlin did not exist or that Marxist-Leninism was a myth. It does indicate that the area of the demonic can become a happy hunting ground for people who prefer to live in a fantasy realm rather than in the real world. This need not be the case, but unfortunately it sometimes is, and such people give "spiritual warfare" a bad name.

A further mistake needs to be mentioned: that of pursuing evil at one level, that is to say of demons, while quite ignoring other dimensions in which the spiritual conflict rages. Although it is hard to credit the power of darkness with too sophisticated a strategy, since its nature is irrational opposition to the good,[1] it could be said that it suits the power of darkness very well if the attention of Christians is fully submerged in occult and demonic concerns, while the wider stage of devilish activity in the political, cultural, national and international spheres is all but ignored.

Trenchant criticisms of the charismatic movement were made along these lines by the Anglo-Catholic theologian Kenneth Leech in his book *The Social God*. He expressed particular concern about the growing preoccupation of "neo-Pentecostalism" with demonology. He pointed out that, in the experience of such people as Dom Robert Petitpierre, possession accounted for only 1 percent of all cases coming forward in this area and that, in the liturgical tradition of the church, exorcism has traditionally been only one part of a "total liturgy of deliverance and healing in which the realm of evil is rejected and man is restored to the divine realm."[2] This serves to put exorcism in its place. But Leech's real concern is that the charismatic approach to evil runs the danger of isolating the demonic from the realm of politics, which he regards as its true home. By doing this the charismatic renewal distorts the "demonic symbol" and tends to "isolate evil within the sphere of the private, and it is this sphere which comes to be seen as par excellence the territory of demons."[3] He fears that concern with demons will actually divert attention from the real conflict with evil in the world and will effectively lead the church into a complacent support of the status quo, rather than being a force for social change. This criticism is one that could be applied to renewal generally, which, along with all forms of pietist religion, might cause people to flee away from engagement with the world into the realm of private ecstatic religious experiences.[4]

I agree with the main thrust of this argument. It is true that charismatic renewal could prove to be an escapist reaction against a harsh and God-rejecting world. It functions in this way in many charismatic churches. The reversal of this process is that charismatic renewal could act as a mighty stimulus and energy source for engagement with the world in evangelism, social and political action, providing spiritual vitality and creativity, as well as the base communities needed to make a social impact.

In relation to the demonic dimensions, it is a matter for specific concern that engagement with afflicted individuals does not so blind our eyes, nor so absorb our attention and energies that we are unable to see and engage the corporate and political activities of the power of darkness. Indeed, we need to be awake to the possibility of diversionary tactics, whereby we become so taken up with a small part of the battle because it is all we can see while the main battle, on a different front, rages without our knowing it.

A theology is needed that puts the individual aspects of the demonic into a much broader context and thereby provides the corrective element. We require a theological map that displays the entire battlefield and prevents us from being taken unawares. We recognize with Walter Wink that "Satan's heart has always been in international politics."[5] According to Revelation 20:3 God will one day "keep him from deceiving *the nations* any more." A shift should take place in our understanding to perceive the involvement of the powers of darkness in the world's power structures. Only then do we see the individual dimensions of the demonic in their true light. The spiritual struggle should be seen on a broader canvas.

It is instructive to describe how a similar shift from the individual to the political was made in a previous generation. In the last chapter the experience of Johann Christoph Blumhardt was described. Through his struggle to set a woman free the impetus was given for a renewal movement, which came to be centered at a conference center at Bad Boll, of which Blumhardt was the leader. The watchword "Jesus is Victor!" characterized this movement, which in some ways parallels the Keswick movement in England, of which the watchword was and is "All One in Christ Jesus!" In 1880 the elder Blumhardt died and was succeeded as leader in Bad Boll by his son Christoph Friedrich Blumhardt (1842-1919), who had imbibed and accepted the hopes and experiences of his father. Christoph was renowned as a mass evangelist and healer.[6] But he became impatient with what he considered the spiritual selfishness of the pious Christians who flocked to Bad Boll.

It should be understood that the Blumhardts were in the tradition of German pietism, an evangelical movement of the seventeenth century, which emphasized, like the English Puritans, the place of experience in the Christian life. Doctrine on its own was not enough; what really mattered was life, the experience of salvation. Standing in this tradition, the Blumhardts nonetheless saw the need to reform it.

The danger of pietism, as with all renewal movements including present ones, was that it could lead to a retreat from the world into egocentric individualism. The Blumhardts advocated the need for a hope that embraced the whole world and looked for the coming of the kingdom of God, which would make all things new. According to Karl Barth:

> They therefore called the world of piety with its apparently very definite faith in Christ, to conversion, to faith in the living Christ who is to come again and make all things new. They gave a central position to the prayer: "Thy Kingdom come" and "Even so, come Lord Jesus," and therefore to post-temporal eternity, although this involved them in a conflict with the most earnest representatives of the anthropocentric Christianity of the Post-Reformation period.[7]

The implications of this approach were dramatic. Christoph Blumhardt's interest took a "turn to the world," and he began to focus on the socioecomonic issues of the day.[8] From 1900 to 1906 he joined the struggle for workers' rights as a Social Democratic deputy in the Stuttgart state parliament—despite the fact that this obliged him to resign his orders as a Lutheran pastor and called down on him the wrath of civil and ecclesiastical authorities. This action was taken at a time when social democracy was strongly Marxist and regarded as extreme. Blumhardt's intention was to bear witness to Christ in the political arena because it was also true there that Jesus was Victor, the bringer of hope.

After six years as an influential deputy he withdrew from the political arena to bear witness to the fact that, although Christ was Lord even in politics, politics itself did not have the answers to the needs of the world. These were to be found in the kingdom of God. Blumhardt's action is an example of how it is possible to be first *responsibly involved* and then *responsibly noninvolved* in the political arena. It was largely out of his witness and thinking that a highly influential movement developed, known as religious socialism, which influenced profoundly several of the major theologians of the twentieth century and large sections of the European political scene.

The point in relating this story is to indicate how renewal movements are inadequate if they only concern themselves with the inner life of Christians. Sooner or later such movements have a tendency to become inward looking unless they engage the world to make a difference in it. The more aware members of such movements, like Blumhardt, begin to feel this and do something about it.

The Blumhardt experience has been paralleled within charismatic circles. Participants begin to feel that it is not good enough for the renewing work of the Spirit to be kept in-house, within the church. It needs to flow out from the church into the world. In recent years there has been a major shift in evangelical thinking and practice toward social action and engagement. In the charismatic movement the focus in spiritual warfare has shifted away from the needs of individuals to the needs of society. In principle this is welcome even if in practice some of the attitudes displayed are questionable. There is a much greater sense of the need to engage the "powers" that rule in our society. This can be discerned in the renewed interest in prayer for society, in events such as the

"Make Way" marches, which are rooted in the philosophy of "claiming territory" for the kingdom of God, and in the politicization that took place surrounding Christian opposition to government legislation on Sunday trading and other laws. It is not the place here to debate the pros and cons of these particular issues but to indicate the heightened awareness of the political dimension in spiritual warfare, which is coming to mark some evangelicals and charismatics. It is good that this is happening, but if it is to happen in a healthy way, there are several points that need to be watched.

First, there is something beguiling about the world of political power that exists as a danger for Christians. In a society where the churches have lost a great deal of their social position and influence, participation in the political process can become a power trip for individuals who enjoy the limelight and the sense of being near to the centers of power. Likewise movements can feel that they grow in significance when they are taken seriously by politicians. There is a line to be drawn here between that sense of being taken seriously as citizens, which is healthy and essential for a participative democracy, and the illegitimate lust for power and influence, which is really a sign of loss of confidence in the church's primary mission.

Second, it must be seen as of primary importance that, in taking a "turn to the world," those Christians who feel called to involve themselves in political action do not become isolated from their roots in the life of the church. Recent history reveals significant numbers of people with Christian backgrounds and commitment who have involved themselves in politics only to find that somewhere along the road their faith has evaporated. This is not always the case at all, but where it does happen the reasons are not difficult to discern. It takes time to sustain any meaningful involvement in the political process. It is possible for church to get squeezed out. Yet the need to combine spirituality and political judgment is acute.

Third, and more important, if the renewal movement in the church is to affect the surrounding community, it will only do this as it develops political philosophies (for want of a better expression) that will enable this to happen. Blumhardt translated his vibrant spiritual experience and hope into a political position (religious socialism) that was appropriate to the circumstances of his day and enabled him to apply the message of hope to his society. There was a time in Britain when Free Church theology went hand in hand with liberal politics. Free Church values were given expression in this way politically and the nonconformist conscience made its mark on the community. We need to find coherent political philosophies that will enable the perspectives for which the church stands to be translated into practical politics. The task of doing this belongs to those who have the ability and training to do it. For this reason it will not be attempted here! It is indeed happening in various ways, for instance through movements for Christian democracy and Christian socialism. I venture here the suggestion that one piece of the jigsaw puzzle must be an analysis of the way in which the power of darkness interacts with the social structures of human communities.

The church has a mission to the world that is comprised of three parts. The first part is evangelistic. We are called to proclaim the good news of the kingdom of God. It calls people to repentance and to a new relationship with the Christ-like God. The second part concerns social action. We embody the love of God in behavior and in communities of faith, caring for people, healing the sick and loving the needy. This is what Christ did. All Christians more or less agree on these parts of the mission, although they may fulfill them in differing ways. The third part is political. It involves living under the lordship of Christ, and this means accepting no other lord, whether this be nation, wealth or political ruler. Christians live for Christ, and if Caesar asks for what belongs to God, so much the worse for Caesar (Mt 22:21)! Christians obey God rather than man (Acts 5:29). Furthermore, Christ is not only head of the church but also head of the universe (Eph 1:20-23; 4:15). All creation owes submission to its Lord. To this end Christians are called to exercise a loving witness to the powers of this world (Eph 3:10-11).

The recognition that the church plays a political role is now widely made, although not with the degree of unanimity that applies in the case of the evangelistic and social aspects of its mission. Yet here is a problem. Christians who agree on the need for political witness disagree radically as to how this ought to be done. An illustration of this is that in presidential elections, two ordained ministers, Pat Robertson and Jesse Jackson, have been among the competitors on opposite sides. Both were rooted in the Christian tradition yet held widely diverging political positions. The essence of the difference between them appeared to be that Robertson stressed personal morality and responsibility while Jackson stressed both the personal and corporate aspects of a moral society. In the media, Baptists, as an example, are often identified with the Religious Right, overlooking the fact that Bill Clinton, regarded as relatively liberal and left wing, is also a Baptist. The same tension is routinely illustrated in politics. It is the recognition that evil is not simply personal but also structural and corporate that leads to different political positions. Put otherwise, the analysis of what is wrong in society determines the political solutions that are advocated. Where what is discerned is failure in personal responsibility and effort, the solution will focus on the individual. Where the emphasis is placed on corrupt and unjust social structures, the solution will be on social reform. However, a true analysis will recognize both personal and corporate dimensions to the problem.

This chapter argues that we should take the social nature of evil seriously without minimizing its individual aspects. In this we agree with Andrew Walker: "It is in the processes and ideologies of the modern world itself that we find the destructive, impersonal and heartless force of the dark Power."[9] This is not to disagree with the saying of Paul that "our struggle is not against flesh and blood" (Eph 6:12) but to say that the form taken by the powers of darkness is not that of free floating or abstract entities that maraud in the heavenlies and attack individuals. They take form and are manifest in the structures of social existence and do their work by afflicting humanity through them. Spiritual struggle cannot be carried on without reference to the actual state of the political, cultural and social context in which we live.

As these statements are of key importance, it is necessary to substantiate them from Scripture. The evidence can be viewed in several ways.

THE BIBLICAL EVIDENCE VIEWED CONCRETELY

It can be argued from the life of Jesus that his conflict with the powers of darkness took form as individual temptation and attack, as well as institutional opposition to him. In the life and death of Jesus we see how evil operates in the world: Jesus is the embodied Word of God, and as such he articulated and demonstrated the revelation of God; in opposition to Christ, we see the nature of evil. Some years ago professor James Stewart drew attention to what was then a neglected emphasis in New Testament studies, namely the element of spiritual conflict in the life of Jesus.[10] In the cross we see the climax of God's self-revelation in Christ, and there are three elements involved in it: the design of human beings, the will of Jesus and the predestination of God. By human design Stewart meant:

> a coalition of ascertainable historical forces. It was the human attitudes of pride, self-love and traditionalism and fear which, when worked out into social, political and ecclesiastical magnitudes resulted in the death of the Son of God.[11]

The coalition consisted of religion, politics and popular opinion. Organized religion was at the cross because it saw itself threatened by Jesus. He was seen as a blasphemer in that he proclaimed and demonstrated the free grace of God toward sinners in a way that overturned the secure, legalistic categories of dominant Jewish religion of the time. He spoke of God's mercy toward the outcast and sinner and embodied this by making friends with the irreligious (Mt 11:19).[12] This was perceived as a major threat to the religious system and drew out the deep hostility of the conventionally religious to Jesus.

A second member of the coalition was politics. Both Jewish and Roman politics had reason to be displeased with Jesus. He had disappointed the hopes of Jewish nationalism because it seemed at first that he might serve the nationalist purpose (Jn 6:15). Equally, he had threatened the totalitarian claims of the Roman system, because it feared any rival to its own power (Lk 23:2; Mt 27:37; Acts 17:7). From both points of view it was expedient to do away with Jesus. If he had been merely a blasphemer it would have been enough to stone him. Because he was also regarded as a rebel he was crucified, the punishment for political offenders.[13]

The third member of the coalition was that of public opinion. The ordinary people, apathetic and easily maneuvered by the more unscrupulous, are represented by the crowd at the cross of Christ (Mk 15:13-14). This represents the demonic power of mob opinion, which can be manipulated in any number of directions according to the occasion.

Social forces are found at the cross. Religious, political and social factors are seen in the crucifying of Jesus to rise up against God in opposition. They show themselves to be antichrist. In the life of Jesus the *modus operandi* of the powers of darkness is revealed. They distort and manipulate the fallen structures of human life for their own end. The spiritual struggle must be carried on in the religious, political and social spheres.

THE BIBLICAL EVIDENCE VIEWED THEOLOGICALLY

This same point can be argued by reference to the theology of the apostle Paul. The focus shifts away from the demonic encounters described in the Gospels to "principalities and powers" (Eph 6:12). Despite the demonic struggles found in the missionary journeys of Paul (Acts 16:16-18; 19:11-16), demons hardly figure at all in Paul's letters.[14] He thinks more broadly about the invisible conflict. It is not immediately clear exactly what Paul had in mind when he referred to these powers. There are three broad lines of interpretation.

1. The first has been popularized since World War II and argues that Paul had in mind the social, political, cultural and religious forces that invisibly shape human existence. Mythological language is used for these realities because it is the only kind that gets to the truth about the invisible world. The language is mythic but the reality is not. There is now a large body of literature arguing this position. A short and influential work in this area was produced under the title *Christ and the Powers* by Hendrik Berkhof.[15] Berkhof evaluated the Pauline language that refers on nine occasions to the "powers."[16] He also discussed references to the *stoicheia* (Col 2:8, 20ff.), the "basic principles" (NIV) or "elemental spirits" (NRSV) of the world, and he sees in all of this language a movement away from notions of personal beings controlling life toward an idea of the "structures of earthly existence."[17] Paul, he thinks, is "demythologizing" supernatural personal powers of good and evil. The powers are the structures of earthly existence created by God (Col 1:16) but are now in a fallen state and hostile to God (Rom 8:38-39). They behave like tyrants and oppress people because they are not subject to God as Lord. Yet one day they will be restored to their proper function in the consummation.[18] The decisive point for Berkhof is that the New Testament envisages a day when the powers will be reconciled to God, and this precludes their being fallen angels.[19] Berkhof doubts that Paul thought of the powers as personal *beings* but as personifications, just as he wrote of sin and death as if they were persons.[20] Others would agree with this judgment. D. E. H. Whiteley states in his standard work on Paul's theology:

I personally believe that, whatever may be said about the demons of the Synoptics, St Paul, consciously or otherwise, was using mythological language. In other words, there are no principalities or powers, but St Paul employs this language to express something which is both true and important.[21]

After exhaustively examining the New Testament data, Walter Wink concludes that the language of power pervades the whole New Testament and is extremely varied, interchangeable and unsystematic. But it refers consistently to genuine power realities, which are heavenly and earthly, divine and human, spiritual and political, invisible and visible, good and evil.[22] Nevertheless, as already noted, the New Testament language is mythic and needs reinterpretation for today in terms of *interiority*, that is "inner aspects of material or tangible manifestations of power." Institutions may be considered to have inner essences or spiritualities, and these are the principalities and powers. Likewise, demons are the psychic or spiritual powers emanated by organizations or individuals—or "subaspects of individuals whose energies are bent on overpowering others."[23] The effect of this is to shift the spiritual battle away from a purely invisible conflict in "the heavenlies" and into the realm of the social, political, religious and cultural realities of our day.

2. Such apparent demythologizing has not commanded universal assent. In particular John Stott has taken a more traditional interpretation of Paul.[24] Stott sees the position taken by Berkhof and others as resulting from embarrassment at the archaic worldview of angels and demons in the New Testament and at the lack of reference to social structures so significant for the modern world. According to Stott, the reinterpreted view of the powers offers us a way of escape from both of these difficulties.[25] He dismisses the "new" approach as failing to do justice to the spiritual conflict "in the heavenlies" of which Paul speaks in Ephesians, and he prefers the traditional interpretation that

the "world rulers of this present darkness" and the "spiritual hosts of wickedness" of Ephesians 6:12 must be taken as supernatural powers, particularly when the context already specifically refers to the devil (vv. 11, 16). To accept the new interpretation is to overthrow a previously almost universal understanding of what these texts mean.

Stott sees three dangers in the new approach. First, without reckoning with the reality of the demonic we have no explanation as to why human structures become tyrannical. Second, we run the danger of restricting our understanding of the devil's activity if we limit it to the structural. Third, we become too negative toward society and its structures if we see them as being evil. In avoiding the deification of structures we end up demonizing them. This said, Stott readily acknowledges that supernatural personal agencies can use structures, traditions, institutions and the like for malevolent purposes as media of their ministry.[26]

3. A third position sees no reason to make these two options mutually exclusive. It cannot credibly be argued that Paul did not really believe in the reality of the devil.[27] Rather, Whiteley must be considered correct when he asserts, "It would seem that St Paul did believe in the real existence of a 'personal' Satan and probably of other personal demons."[28] We have touched on the question of what "personal" might mean, and we have no way of pursuing this discussion with Paul himself!

However, there appears no reason why the language of the powers could not also be taken to refer to the structures of human existence. This would appear to be warranted for the following reasons. First, there is clearly an ambiguity in Paul's language such that certain references could be taken either to refer to earthly or to spiritual powers. Michael Green writes: "The truth of the matter is that words like principalities, powers and thrones are used both of human rulers and of the spiritual forces which lie behind them."[29] He concludes there is deliberate ambiguity, particularly evident in 1 Corinthians 2:8: "None of the rulers of this age understood it, for if they had, they would not have crucified the Lord of glory." Green stresses the need "to realise the flexibility of such terms as principalities and powers in the usage of the New Testament. They do, on occasion, refer to human authorities. They do, for the main part, refer to superhuman agencies in the spiritual world."[30]

Wink, for reasons that can be seen to accord with his overall proposal, also recognizes the ambiguity of the language and argues it to be deliberately fluid, comprehending spiritual and political, invisible and structural realities.[31] This is further confirmed by Markus Barth, who comments: "The principalities and powers are at the same time intangible spiritual entities and concrete historical, social or psychic structures or institutions of all created things and all created life."[32]

We are not obliged to agree with John Stott that the New Testament has nothing to say about social structures, or that the position outlined here represents an "uneasy compromise."[33] The point is precisely that the power structures of human life are vulnerable and open to invasion by the powers of darkness, or, indeed, that it is out of the powers of darkness and the fallen human beings from whom they operate that a *spiritual* dynamic is generated. It is through the powers that a distorted spiritual power exercises its hold. The issue at stake is whether this reality is implied in Paul's theology or is being read back in. Stott denies it is envisaged in Scripture but accepts its reality in actual experience. However, a close connection between the power structures of society and the powers of darkness which create enslavement and exploitation accords with the ambiguous way power language is used in the New Testament.

There is therefore no contradiction between Paul's theology and the concrete experience of Jesus. Indeed, Paul is explicating, here as in other places, what is visible in the life of Christ. As religion, politics and popular opinion were used to crucify the Son of God, the powers of darkness taking form within them, so Paul speaks of the powers and principalities that threaten human life. He makes explicit what is to be perceived in the life of Jesus. As his doctrine of justification by faith explains in theological terms the actions of Jesus befriending sinners, so it is with the powers. He expounds the concrete experience of Jesus in his encounter with evil, an experience repeated in the life of the church. We may not wish to demythologize the devil, but at the very least these insights augment our understanding of how the powers of darkness work. As Green puts it:

> Inflation and unemployment, the arms race and the corruption of morals, these are all manifestations in the modern state of principalities and powers. The state does not want these things, for the most part. It struggles hard to get rid of them. But it fails. It is in the grip of a power beyond its own.[34]

This does not demonize structures but recognizes that they enhance or distort human existence according to the power that is at work within them.

THE BIBLICAL EVIDENCE VIEWED APOCALYPTICALLY

A third cross-sectional view is in the apocalyptic imagery of the book of Revelation, particularly chapters 12—13. Here an unholy triad is set up against God and his people in the form of the dragon (Rev 12:3), the beast out of the sea (Rev 13:1) and the beast out of the earth (Rev 13:12). The dragon represents Satan, as is clear from Revelation 13:9; the beast out of the sea is the power of Rome that blasphemously claims supremacy; the beast out of the earth represents the religious system of the Empire, the false spirituality, which is devoted to the worship of the emperor.

Behind the whole system of totalitarian power and false religion is the manipulative power of evil (Rev 13:2). Here, "the struggle of the saints against the Caesars is portrayed in the context of an age-long resistance to the God of heaven on the part of evil powers."[35] The evil power takes form in the political and religious structures of the Roman Empire. The opposition to God's people is shown in a combination of political and ideological hostility. This does not mean that the state is intrinsically evil. According to Romans 12:4 it is "God's servant for your good." But at times, the state has become demonized, and indeed, it is always in danger of doing so if it goes beyond its proper function of serving humankind to the point where it makes itself of ultimate concern. In some countries, the totalitarian perversion of the state is obvious. In others it is concealed but will be brought out the moment the vested interests of the powerful are threatened.

Although expressed apocalyptically, that is in symbolic and seemingly lurid terms, the picture here is in line with that discerned in Paul's theological statements and the concrete circumstances of Jesus' life. The emerging picture from all three cross-sectional views is of a world in which the invisible realities that determine and shape life consist of spiritual and structural powers. The structures reflect and participate in the fallen state of the human race. They reflect human sin and compound the problem, yet are not intrinsically evil. Having been made by God they will one day be redeemed and will resume their proper function (Col 1:15-20).

In the meantime they can be humanized, at least to a degree, and brought back into line in order to serve and not oppress. The powers that at the moment operate as if they were a law unto themselves need to be helped to see that they too have a Lord. They can no longer function as if they were lordless powers. It is here that our spiritual concern needs to be recognized. To be truly spiritual the powers need to be willingly and wholeheartedly directed toward the true Lord. To the extent that they are not they are the arena of a false spirituality.

As an illustration of this we highlight one issue. There is the insidious danger of nationalism. It is natural for people to love their country and to appreciate its strengths. Nationhood can serve to draw people together in cooperative action beyond the sectionalism of family and tribal self-interest. But the perversion of a proper love of country is nationalism, whereby the nation's interests assume a godlike status. When this happens we are in danger of being controlled by a power that has become demonic. This is all the more threatening when nationalism harnesses religion to its own ends, as it almost invariably seeks to do, and as did the Roman Empire. This was abundantly clear when Hitler tried to domesticate the church in the interests of National Socialism. The same trend can be discerned in the United States, where Christianity and Americanism are closely identified. Christianity is in danger of losing its power by being harnessed to the interests of the nation, perpetuating a myth of national purity and righteousness, a kind of imperialistic fundamentalism that is incapable of self-criticism.

As an example, this was clearly visible in the Congressional hearings surrounding Lieutenant Colonel Oliver North during the Reagan years. It is well to recall it before the historical memory fades. North, a charismatic Christian, was offended to the core when accused of irregularity in his private life. But he proudly confessed to being ready to lie, deceive, kill and maim in the name and for the sake of America. The interests of the country and the Christian cause were clearly identified. What would be unthinkable to him in one sphere was perfectly possible in another. It is obvious that this is a distorted perspective. When such a thing happens, Christians should take warning. There is a beguiling, deceptive power at work that has the ability to ensnare Christians and make them prisoners of their nation, their social class or their interest group.

Until and unless Christians perceive this and resolve not to be conformed to the world but to be transformed, radically renewed in the image of Christ, they are fooling themselves that they are engaged in spiritual warfare. Indeed, outrage at the rise of the occult, prayer marches and attempts to bind the powers of darkness could all be one major deception and diversion if we fail to appreciate the subtlety of the issues at stake. While believing self-righteously that we are living for God in one area we could in fact be selling out completely in another. The key to all of this is our ability to recognize the form that evil can take in the world's corporate structures and the difficulty we have in perceiving it. This requires understanding and discernment on our part, in addition to the ability to think as well as pray.

Unless we recognize the dual aspect of the powers, the spiritual and the structural, we may miss the point. The solution does not lie in prayer alone. We must see the way in which the power of darkness interacts with and draws strength from the investment that fallen people and structures make to it. It is not only that there are spiritual forces that need to be ejected from the structure. There are powerful elements of the structure itself that compounds the strength of the power of darkness. The two are symbiotic. One grows as the other does. If we use the weapon of prayer to confound the spiritual power of darkness, it simply reappears again, unless we deal with a major source of its energy in the matrix of human life. Here we express again the idea that the power of darkness actually grows and increases to the extent to which "faith" is given to it.

TERRITORIAL SPIRITS

We have previously referred to the development in spiritual warfare, which moves from thinking about demonization to an analysis of corporate evil in the form of "territorial spirits," demonic spirits and fallen angels that exercise geographical control over cities and regions. As an early example of this, at the Dales Bible Week in 1977 at the Harrogate Showground, Yorkshire, England, Ern Baxter (one of the "Fort Lauderdale Five" who were influential at the time) first expounded the nature of the demonic kingdom as a hierarchical structure. He then invited those present to "intelligently and purposefully" bind a powerful, national evil spirit called the "prince of Great Britain" and to "paralyse the power of that dark-winged spirit that hovers over the Parliament building." In addition the claim was made that "We're going to deal with subsidiary deputies. We're going to send demons scrambling for cover as Jesus Christ is declared King of Great Britain." After prayer had been offered, members of the assembly were invited to "deliver your own town" by means of similar prayers.[36] We may be left to judge whether any significant changes came about through this action but, personally, I doubt it.

It would be deduced rightly from this book so far that I am not sympathetic to the notion of territorial spirits, regarding it as subjective and uncontrolled both biblically and theologically. I see it as a mythologizing of the powers and principalities and, as such, a diversion.[37] It is another attempt to find a technique for success in evangelism. There is, however, a residue of truth in it and this is to do with the "atmospheres" that are constellated (to borrow a term from Walter Wink) in places, cultures and countries by the powers—atmospheres that are open to or resistant to God's grace and which are the accumulated product of all the energies that have led up to them. In this sense it is possible to discern a kind of spirituality at work in the many cultures we produce. We are shaped by these atmospheres but also have the capacity to change them through our actions and our prayers. By developing, in Christian communities, centers of truly Christian spirituality, centered on worship of the triune God and on discipleship of Jesus Christ, we "constellate" an alternative and godly spirituality that has the potential to subvert the false gods, to provide communities of resistance to their encroaching spirituality, and to open up the spiritual atmosphere to the gracious and healing presence of the living God.

Spiritual struggle must therefore be carried on simultaneously on two fronts: through prayer and through persuasive action. In prayer the power of the kingdom of God is given access to human life. In persuasive action men and women and institutions are called to invest in what is good and true rather than what is wrong and false. These two constitute the spirituality that undergirds our spiritual struggle as we take seriously the spiritual dimensions of the human dilemma and the structural forms and distortions that are produced by the world, the flesh and the devil in coalition.

CHAPTER EIGHT

DE-DEMONIZING
CREATION

The task we now attempt should probably have been done before. We are concerned to show how the power of darkness has been overcome in Jesus Christ. It may well be that this chapter should've been the first to be written. After all, we have been keen to demonstrate that the power of darkness must be kept in its place. The concern has been to develop a way of thinking about evil that takes it seriously but does not let it get out of hand. The power of darkness is inherently deceptive and keen to convince us it is overwhelming, all pervading and worthy of our attention. What better way to counteract this than to show from the very beginning that its power is a negated power, an enemy overcome in Christ? For the Christian, the mere thought of the power of darkness should be immediately accompanied by the knowledge that it has met its match and been trodden under foot by Jesus.

That we have delayed consideration of how Christ has gained the victory until now is a question of method. Is it better to outline the problem before dealing with the solution or the other way around? In favor of focusing on the negative before accentuating the positive is that to know the size of the problem helps to appreciate the solution when it comes. First the bad news, then the good news. Conversely, to begin with the victory of Christ means that any subsequent investigation of evil is bathed in the light of that victory, and evil is defined by what Christ has already achieved. From the outset, therefore, the power of darkness is seen in true perspective and kept firmly where it belongs in our thoughts, under the heel of the "Victor." Nevertheless, we have chosen to move from the negative to the positive but have wished from the start to show that the defeat of evil by Christ undergirds our entire investigation. The task now is to consider how the victory was gained and how it may be held to alter the circumstances of the world in which we live.

Earlier we commented on the origin of the slogan "Jesus is Victor!" in the experience of the elder Blumhardt. The New Testament presents us with the picture of a triumphant Christ, who through humiliation and suffering did what was necessary to overcome the power of evil. To illustrate this we refer to various strands of the New Testament witness where the point is made abundantly clear.

- In the *Synoptic strand* is Jesus' reference to binding the strong man so that his possessions may be plundered and carried off (Mt 12:29). This occurs in the context of Jesus' healing of the demonized. He is accused by the Pharisees of doing so by the power of Beelzebub, the prince of demons (v. 24). Jesus replies that he drives out Satan by the Spirit of God and this is the sign that the kingdom of God has begun to come. There is one stronger than the strong man, namely the Holy Spirit, by whose power at work in Jesus the demons are expelled.[1]

- The *Johannine strand* reflects a similar understanding of the work of Christ but sees the defeat of evil being accomplished in the cross. "Now is the judgment of this world; now the ruler of this world will be driven out. And I, when I am lifted up from the earth, will draw all people to myself" (Jn 12:31-32). The train of thought here is that the world's situation is changed by the lifting up of Jesus Christ on the cross. The dethroning of Satan is accompanied by the enthroning of Christ over the world he died to save.[2] In this saying of Jesus there are echoes of Luke 10:18, "I saw Satan fall like lightning from heaven," and of course 1 John 3:8, "The reason the Son of God appeared was to destroy the devil's work."

- The *Pauline strand* is well represented by Colossians 2:9-15 where the work of Christ is portrayed as a clear victory over the powers and authorities. Christ is the head of every power and authority (2:10). Having died on the cross he has canceled the legal record of our sins that "was against us and stood opposed to us" (v. 14). Moreover, he "disarmed the rulers and authorities and made a public example of them, triumphing over them in it [the cross]" (v. 15).

  Paul moves from forgiveness of sins to the victory of the cross since it is through the guilt of men and women that the dark powers are able to hold them in bondage. Once this guilt is removed by atonement, the hold of the powers is broken. The picture is of a victory parade in which the conquered powers are drawn along in God's triumphal procession and paraded as enemies who have been overcome and whose rule is over. They are unwilling servants of Christ, though they may continue to be hostile, but they have been overcome. And their ultimate overthrow is sure and certain—although still future.[3]

- The *Petrine strand* of testimony is discerned in 1 Peter 3:18-22, which again brings together the work of Christ on the cross and the victory he now enjoys. Christ has "suffered for sins once for all." He has been "put to death in the flesh but made alive by the Spirit" (v. 18). He has proclaimed his victory to the imprisoned spirits (v. 19) and is now in heaven at God's right hand "with angels, authorities, and powers made subject to him" (v. 22). Here the victory of Christ is achieved in the resurrection, through which he has been raised above the spiritual powers that opposed him. In this way the evil powers have been shattered.[4]

- The final testimony to which we refer is that of the *Apocalyptic strand*, particularly to the highly colored vision of Revelation 12. In this we see a scene of conflict. The dragon persecutes from his birth the Messiah who is born of the messianic people, but God raises him to his very throne (v. 5). The dragon represents the devil working through the power of the Roman Empire (compare v. 7 with v. 3). Michael and his angels (representing the forces of God) fight against the dragon who is hurled down with his angels to the earth. But the conquest of the devil is made possible "by the blood of the Lamb and by the word of their testimony" (v. 11). In other words, "it is the redemptive death and resurrection of the Christ confessed in the gospel (the 'testimony') which has conquered the devil."[5]

Here in the apocalyptic language of the Revelation is clear testimony to the victory of Christ. The victory has been gained through the blood of Christ. In Revelation 5 this is strikingly illustrated in John's vision of God. The only one found worthy to open the scroll of human destiny is the Lion of Judah: "Do not weep. See, the Lion of the tribe of Judah, the Root of David, has conquered, so he can open the scroll and its seven seals. Then I saw . . . a Lamb, standing as if it had been slaughtered" (Rev 5:5-6). The Lion of Judah is also the Lamb of God. It is through his sacrificial work as the Lamb of God who takes away the sins of the world that Jesus Christ has become the victorious Lion of Judah.

We could go on amassing the biblical evidence to demonstrate that the work of Christ is portrayed as victory over hostile powers, but the case is sufficiently proved. The unequivocal testimony is that Jesus is Victor. In view of this, Christian theology has made much use of the idea of victory in describing the work of Christ. Over fifty years ago a book was published by the Swedish theologian Gustaf Aulén (1879-1977), which aimed to recapture the concept of atonement as victory. He argued that recent thought had understood atonement either through the "satisfaction" approach associated with Anselm or through the "subjective" approach associated with Abelard. One saw Christ's work as satisfying God's honor (or God's wrath in Calvin's parallel version). The other understood it in terms of its ability to influence sinners toward the good.

In preference, Aulén advocated the renewal of the concept of victory to explain the cross. Christ—*Christus Victor*—fights against and triumphs over the powers of the world, the "tyrants" under which humankind is in bondage, and in Christ, God reconciles the world to himself.[6]

Aulén describes this as the "classic idea" and the "dramatic view" of the atonement,[7] which has fallen into neglect in Christian thinking despite being the fundamental motif for understanding the work of Christ. Its strength is that it definitely sees atonement as God's work and avoids the alleged anthropocentric or legalistic approaches of the other theories. It is the characteristic teaching of the New Testament,[8] of the early church fathers—especially of Irenaeus[9]—and of Martin Luther. Luther argued that humanity was imprisoned by the tyrants of sin, death, the devil, wrath and the law, and he argued that Christ overcame them all.[10] He saw the work of Christ as one of deliverance brought about by God in the drama of the death and resurrection of Christ. Aulén's thesis has been criticized from a number of angles but is basically sound so far as it goes, though he might be faulted for implying that the classic idea excludes any other description or is to be preferred above them. In fact, if Christ has won a victory on the cross, it must be because he made an atonement there that propitiated the wrath of God and expiated our sin. As Paul Althaus has written:

> The satisfaction which God's righteousness demands constitutes the primary and decisive significance of Christ's work and particularly of his death. Everything else depends on this satisfaction, including the destruction of the might and authority of the demonic powers.[11]

Despite this qualification Aulén is accurate in stressing the dramatic context in which the atoning work of the cross is set and of which it is the decisive moment. It is by the blood of Christ poured out for sinners that guilt is removed and bondage is broken. It is to announce and reveal this breaking of Satan's power, this finished work, that Christ is raised from the dead and enthroned as king over all. The retelling of this drama and conquest is the concern of the church. Indeed it is with this story that the whole Bible is concerned. John Stott sees six stages in this drama. It is *predicted* in the Old Testament. It is *begun* in the ministry of Jesus as demons are dismissed, sicknesses healed and disordered nature acknowledges its Lord. It is *achieved* at the cross where the prince of this world is driven out. It is *confirmed* and announced in the resurrection when the victory of the cross was endorsed, proclaimed and demonstrated. It is *extended* as the church preaches Christ in the power of the Holy Spirit. It will be *consummated* when Christ returns and makes his victory universal and total.[12] From this perspective of an accomplished work, the Christian views and considers the still-active power of darkness. Though active, its days are numbered and its doom sealed.

There are other ways in which we may recount the story. The gospel is fundamentally a story that recounts a pattern of creation, fall, redemption, extension and consummation. Within this context we may understand the history and future of the human race and of those powers and principalities, which, although invisible, are strikingly real.

CREATION

According to Colossians 1:16, in Christ "all things in heaven and on earth were created, things visible and invisible, whether thrones or dominions or rulers or powers—all things have been created through him and for him." Whatever we understand by powers and principalities and however we explain the disorder that now marks them we cannot escape the fact that they are created realities. They have come into being through the creative work of God in Christ without whom "nothing was made that has been made" (Jn 1:3). In Romans 8:38 the powers are numbered among created things. They are created realities that owe their origin to God along with the rest of creation. Whatever we conclude about the ontological status of the devil we remember that, whatever the devil is, he does not and cannot exist independently of the God who created all. Even he must trace his existence to the Creator even if this existence, as we have argued, is constructed parasitically out of fallen humanity as its ontological ground. We live in a world that has come from God and exists because of his decision to let things be.

FALL

Colossians 1:19-20 goes on to speak of the day when all things will be reconciled to God. Implicit in this passage is an event or a series of events of dislocation or alienation from God's creative intention. Here, as indeed in all the Bible, "a cosmic rupture of enormous proportions"[13] is implied. We have noted how the human Fall is placed center stage in this rupture (Gen 3:1-24; Rom 5:12-21). The idea of a *pre-human* cosmic fall, an aberration in the created world, is only gently hinted at, if at all. Colossians 2:15 speaks of the need for powers and authorities to be disarmed, implying a cosmic conflict in an invisible realm. It is clear that something has happened to bring this about. In view of previous discussions concerning the lordless powers, in which we have argued that New Testament terms are fluid and include the spiritual and the structural, we need to conceive of this disruption in three stages, which have taken place either swiftly or gradually, to create this rupture.

Although cautious about the notion of an "angelic catastrophe," we have found room for the idea of some disruption in the created sphere as the emerging creation, existing under the pressure of collapse back into chaos, experiences distortion and diversion in its development. We have distinguished however between the Shadow and Nothingness and seen the complexities of disentangling the two. We also noted suggestions that the world of nature may have been "subjected" to in its development in advance of the Fall of humanity.

The second stage of the cosmic rupture is clearer since, placed into a world in which they experience anxiety, human beings fall short of their vocation to trust in and obey God, and they fall prey to temptation and testing, exalting themselves in the place of God. This is unmistakably the message of Genesis 3. This signals the entry into the human race of the power of death and darkness, which increases its own power now that it may feed parasitically on estranged human life, bloating itself on the lifeblood that it sucks out. It thrives on the attention it receives and magnifies itself. This effectively marks the moment at which the devil as a powerful adversary begins to be constructed. The devil

> is not impersonal like stones or bureaucracies: he is a non-person. The Devil has become all that God is not: he is not beyond personality—he is without it. His purpose in creation is not to destroy God; he knows that he cannot do that. He wants to draw us into the vortex of non-personhood that he has become, and the nothingness of non-being that he is becoming. Satan, in short, aims to take as many of us with him as he can.[14]

The third stage in the drama of disruption involves the fall in and with the human race of those created elements of human life that were intended to give shape and order to human society: the "powers." As human beings have emancipated themselves from God, so their own possibilities now emancipate themselves from them. Thinking that they are lords over their own lives they are actually the prisoners of created forces that have become disorderly. The powers that we have already referred to as social, political, religious and cultural begin to dominate. Paul says that there are many gods and many lords that paradoxically are nothing (1 Cor 8:5). Yet they claim humanity's allegiance. Jesus warned of the god of money that he called Mammon (Mt 6:24; Lk 16:13). It rivaled the true God. No doubt Jesus never thought that there actually was a god called Mammon, but he recognized the almost controlling and directive way in which money claimed loyalty and pushed people in an unrighteous direction (Lk 16:11 RSV).

In some of his last work Karl Barth was to write of the powers that have fallen in and with humankind.[15] He describes how in Goethe's poem *The Sorcerer's Apprentice* human capacities become spirits with a life of their own, and he sees in this an illustration of how humankind's possibilities take on their own momentum and become the motors of society. If humankind slips out of God's service

> he thereby forfeits the lordship that should be his. In the sudden or gradual movement with which man breaks free from God, he revolutionizes the natural forces that are coordinated with him. . . . It is he who is at the helm, who pulls the levers, who presses the knobs. Nevertheless, they automatically and autonomously rumble and work and roll and roar and clatter outside him, without him, past him and over him. He finds that he himself is subject to their law which he has foreseen, and to their power, which he has released. Turning aside from God, he is himself displaced, that is, jerked out of his proper position in relation to these forces into one that is unworthy of him. Still his slaves, they now confront him as robots which he himself has to serve, and not without being forced to fear their possible pranks.[16]

In Barth's picture, human beings first displace God and then are displaced by their own possibilities. The powers and principalities arise out of the created human potential to build communities, institutions, traditions, practices, structures, nations and all else. Yet these powers declare their independence and begin to rule over those to whom they should be subject. It is in this negatively and chaotically constructed space, derived from the conscious and unconscious energies of an ever-growing and technologically expanding and fatally flawed humanity, that we are now to look for the devil and his angels. For whatever latent possibilities there are in creation and in humans for chaos and mischief are now magnified beyond measure. Here then is a description of the fallen state that has produced the destructive disorder that now "bedevils" us. It can clearly be seen to consist of those three enemies that are familiar to the Christian church—the flesh, which is our fallen humanity; the world, which is our rebellious and stubborn corporate existence; and the devil, which is the malicious and destructive spirituality produced as an epiphenomenon out of this chaotic cocktail.

A more modern metaphor than Barth's might be found in the 1990s cult film *The Matrix*. According to the film human beings invent artificial intelligence that proves to be so successful that it wars against and displaces human beings in order to enslave them. But artificial intelligence cannot exist without human beings since they are its source of energy and so must breed them in human being farms and then parasitically draw on them. To keep them complacent it constructs a virtual, computer-generated reality according to which humans are deluded into believing that life continues unchanged. This is the matrix, and it is kept in place by "agents" who deal with any breech of the illusion. *The Matrix* is an imaginative fantasy about a world constructed out of human life and technology, which then achieves dominance over the very creatures from which it is derived—and from which the humans need liberation by a Messiah who knows the truth and can set them free.

REDEMPTION

The redeeming work of Christ needs to take account of the condition that we have just described. It must provide the solution to the Fall in its three stages or dimensions of world, flesh and devil. We consider how Christ has overcome each of the enemies.

Overcoming the world. "But take heart! I have overcome the world" said Jesus (Jn 16:33). This seemed a strange thing to say and a strange time to say it! Jesus was on the verge of being crucified, how then could he overcome the world? Yet we are faced with the fact that the apparent defeat of the cross is portrayed as a victory. What kind of victory is this? It is the victory of one who, unlike all others, refuses to be dominated by the powers that have been let loose in the world through the Fall and which now control humankind. Walter Wink describes this world of powers and principalities as "the Domination System."[17] Christ does not submit to the System but lives as a free child of God. He acknowledges the Father's authority above and beyond all powers. The idolatrous concerns of worldly power, legalistic religion and human popularity are unable to dominate him and so conspire to destroy him.

In the temptation narrative described in Luke 4:1-12, Satan offers Jesus the possibility of worldly success and influence, and this is equivalent to worshiping Satan (v. 9). But Jesus resists Satan and overcomes him. He lives in obedience to God and rejects idolatry—which means making someone or something other than God his ultimate concern. He does in the wilderness what Adam failed to do in the Garden. Despite being pressured, tested and tempted he finds his security not in self-exaltation or self-indulgence but in trusting in the living God. In doing this Jesus breaks the domination of the world and overcomes it. He breaches the dike of human conformity and disobedience. In this light, the cross of Christ is the ultimate act of refusal to conform. Even under extreme duress and though his life is taken he refuses to depart from the way of obedience to God.

> Only in a very restricted sense is it right to understand the cross as submission—as a man's free submission to the dark powers that would destroy him. The submission is depicted, for example, in the Fourth Gospel, as an active exercise of authority: it is a submission that consists in the refusal to submit.[18]

In this way, Christ pioneers for the whole of humanity, in solidarity and communion with himself, through his risen life the possibility of life free from the domination of the world and its powers. We are able to live in him as those who are free at last.

Overcoming the flesh. "For Christ died for sins once for all, the righteous for the unrighteous, to bring you to God" (1 Pet 3:18). When we speak of Christ's death for the human race we are speaking of the crucial and pivotal moment in the work of redemption. Christ fulfills his work by participating in our humanity and taking on himself what is ours in order that what is his may become ours. An exchange takes place (2 Cor 5:21). He died in place of all and for the sake of all. He bore our sins so as to be "the Lamb of God who takes away the sin of the world" (Jn 1:29). In this way God himself in gracious love provides the means whereby the wrath we bring on ourselves may be propitiated and our sin expiated. Guilt being atoned for, we may be reconciled with God through Christ. By the work of the Spirit this becomes a reality. It means that people can be changed from within, overcoming the compulsive drives of sin, crucifying the old downward drag of our distorted natures and creating holy living in the energy that God gives. The message of the cross of Christ has the power of God for salvation. It releases into us that power that judges and buries our old life and awakens and opens up a new one. The flesh is therefore overcome.

Overcoming the devil. "Now the prince of this world will be driven out" (Jn 12:31). The cross of Christ has removed the source of the devil's domination of the human race. It is because we were alienated from God and guilty before him that the power of darkness had sway over us. Once guilt has been atoned for and reconciliation accomplished there is no longer any ground on which the accuser may oppress human beings. Reconciled to God, we are able to live free of the domination of idols and, in fellowship with Christ, offer ourselves up to the Father to do his good pleasure. This very fact is accomplished in the cross, resurrection and ascension of Christ, which sees him lifted up above the earth and then above every power and authority. At God's right hand Christ has supreme authority and is ruling over the processes of time and history until he has put all his enemies under his feet (1 Cor 15:25).

God is heavily into *perestroika*, restructuring! The events of cross and resurrection speak of a fundamental alteration in the spiritual conflict whereby Christ has conquered the devil, sin and the alienated structures of the world. It is this victory that is the cause of Christian confidence when faced with the continuing reality of the power of darkness.

EXTENSION

All that we have already said brings us up to date. We are currently living in the time that follows the victory of Christ and that precedes the age of final victory. For this reason the spiritual conflict appears more intense than ever. In the language of the book of Revelation, the devil has been cast down from heaven to earth and the battle is at its fiercest (12:12). The fact that evil is very active is not a sign that its power has not been conquered but that having been vanquished it knows that its time is short and therefore is engaged in intense struggle.

In the period of extension, the task of the church is to see the kingdom of God that came in and with Jesus spreading throughout the world. The kingdom of God will be seen in the casting out of Satan (Lk 11:10), the rescuing of people from sin and guilt (Col 1:13) and the humanizing of human society so that it may serve God and humanity in the orderly fashion that is its proper function (Eph 1:20-21; Phil 2:10-11; 1 Cor 15:24-25). We do not pretend that any of this is easy. The language of conflict and warfare often seems appropriate to this struggle. According to Paul, "We must go through many hardships to enter the kingdom of God" (Acts 14:22). There are struggles with the devil, the world and the flesh, and none of them is easy. There is no room for triumphalism, the easy celebration of victory or superiority. But there is room for, and a need of, the underlying sense of confidence and triumph, of a victory that has already been won and that will one day be complete, to sustain us in the task.

In the period of extension of the kingdom of God, Christians need a proper sense of the "even now" and the "not yet." The kingdom has come and is among us; therefore we may expect evidence of its presence and power. It is present as a dynamic force, which means that tomorrow has already broken into today. We have a foretaste of what is to be and signs of the coming reality. Still, the kingdom is not yet. It is not fully come and manifest. We only know in part or possess in part. We will have enough now to sustain us but not enough completely to satisfy us or leave us feeling there is nothing more to hope for. Christian existence is peculiar in that it is caught between here and there, present and future, strength and weakness, success and failure, cross and resurrection. When we are tempted to despair we need to remember that it was not in spite of but *through* Gethsemane and Golgotha that the world's redemption was achieved. Christians too are called to share in Christ's sufferings for the world and to await the day of resurrection.

CONSUMMATION

But the day will come. The morning will dawn and the sun of righteousness shall rise with healing in its wings (Mal 4:2). The whole Bible points toward the day when God will be supreme in this world. The Jewish people as a whole have always found it difficult to accept that Jesus is the Messiah. In their interpretation, when the Messiah comes he comes to put things right, to bring in the age of justice and mercy and to abolish the darkness. Christ came, but the darkness continues. How then can he be the Messiah?

Some Jews, at the time of Jesus, attempted to interpret the diverse Old Testament passages that referred to the coming of Messiah by teaching that two Messiahs would come. One would be a suffering Messiah, fulfilling the servant songs recorded in Isaiah. The other would be a great king who would come and rule, fulfilling the expectation of a Davidic king (Ezek 37:18-28). Christians do not believe in two Messiahs who come once but in one Messiah who comes twice. Christ came as the Lamb to atone. He will come again as the Lion (but a lion who is still defined as the Lamb) to complete and to consummate the work he has already achieved. Having reordered and created in his first coming, he is now by the Spirit transforming the world until it is brought into complete and universal harmony (Eph 1:9-10; Col 2:19-20). Christians see the whole world moving to this day, this "christological Omega," not smoothly as if in a steady and measurable progression but through the conflict and struggle that belong to the present age.

The power of darkness has been put in its place by Jesus Christ. Although it enjoys a measure of vitality, it is comprehended and controlled by God, who is working out his purpose. Gustaf Aulén completed his classic work on the atonement with the words:

> For my own part, I am persuaded that no form of Christian teaching has any future before it except such as can keep steadily in view the reality of the evil in the world, and go to meet it with the battle-song of triumph.[19]

Because of the de-demonizing of the world by Christ, the breaking of the power of darkness, we are able to do just this in anticipation of the day when all the world shall be free at last.

CHAPTER NINE

THE LOVE OF POWER AND THE POWER OF LOVE

Because we are in a spiritual battle the language of military conflict is appropriate. The Son of God came to destroy the works of the devil. The church of God is wrestling with the opposing forces of darkness. We are to put on the armor of God. The book of Revelation describes war in heaven. The world is moving toward the final spiritual conflict in the last battle called Armageddon. Besides these New Testament references the language of conflict comes easily to those who are acquainted with the many battles of the Old Testament and the picture of God as a warrior. The language of war helps us to describe our Christian experience. We fight against temptations, trials, difficulties and against the evil that is within us and beyond us. Few Christians have escaped the poignant sense of the need to "win" and to overcome the obstacles that are placed in the way. From these facts we conclude that warfare language has a useful and indeed necessary part to play.

Battle imagery makes periodic comebacks in the church's vocabulary. We are the church militant. It is common to sing songs about being Christian soldiers, the army of the Lord, taking the land, possessing the fruit, wielding the sword. One Christian movement, the Salvation Army, has made the military metaphor its defining motif. We are ready to bind the enemy, to march for Jesus, to trample on the devil, to call the powers to bow down. The clenched fist, as well as the open upraised hand, has become a sign of the charismatic movement in the church. The raised voice, authoritative command and the aggressive posture toward an invisible enemy is now part of our stock in trade.

Once Christians were the "quiet in the land" who kept a low profile, busied themselves with their own affairs and endeavored, as far as they could, to live peacefully with all. Unfortunately, this attitude also meant that they were inclined to be conformists and allowed evil to triumph while good people did nothing. The evangelical withdrawal from political and social engagement, which has more recently been seen as a major fault, was a direct outgrowth of the view that the root of all problems was the need for individual transformation. More recently we have been inclined to see that the changing of the individual must be accompanied by the transformation of the social context if we are to do justice to the gospel of the kingdom rather than simply one of personal salvation. Indeed the mood has now so changed that Christians are on the move politically and have consciously entered the political fray.

I recall a pivotal moment in this change of mood. It was after the upheavals of the 1960s, which were marked by riots, strikes, student sit-ins and demonstrations. It was a response to the onset of the permissive society, the upsurge of pornography and the casting aside of traditional sexual restraints. It surfaced in the Festival of Light in 1971 when thousands of slogan-shouting, sticker-bearing, placard-waving Christians marched around London and demonstrated for Jesus against sin. It was a heady occasion when Christians realized that they were not a tiny, insignificant minority, but had muscle. They could muster large crowds of highly motivated individuals with relative ease. We had power after all, and we were going on the offensive. At the same time, I could not help feeling then that we were in danger of playing the world at its own game. We were flexing our muscles and taking to the streets in the same way we had seen others do, of whom we disapproved.

The language of battle is not without its dangers. It also contains a huge challenge. This is true of any language that we apply to God. All God talk proceeds by analogy, using the language of the visible and known to describe the invisible and unknown. Of course it is only in the dynamic of God's self-revelation that we know which human words and concepts are appropriate and which are not. But there is a point at which every analogy breaks down or requires extensive redefinition for it not to be misunderstood. There comes a point at which we can only use it if we also qualify it. If we do not correct the vocabulary of war and aggression with (for instance) that of peace and suffering love, we find ourselves spinning off on to a world of ungodly attitudes.

On the human level war is a cruel business, and to wage it effectively, people have to make themselves nasty. You cannot stick a bayonet into somebody in love. To do it you have to be filled with hate, fear, aggression. The adrenaline has to be flowing to make you do something that under normal conditions you never would. The experience of war indicates that once a war posture has been struck it is very difficult to control. The violence escalates. War cannot be strictly controlled or targeted against an exact aggressor. Despite the arrival of smart bombs, laser-guided delivery and the fantasy that this time we can target the people we really are against, innocent civilians get caught up in it. Soldiers die in friendly fire. Atrocities are committed by all sides. The engine of anger goes on running even when it is no longer needed. War brings every other evil in its train.

> Does not war demand that almost everything that God has forbidden be done on a broad front? To kill effectively, must not those who wage war steal, kill, rob, commit arson, lie, deceive, slander and unfortunately also to a large extent fornicate, not to speak of the almost inevitable repression of all the finer and weightier forms of obedience?[1]

Once Christians adopt the language, mentality and posture of spiritual war they are doing a necessary thing but also a risky thing, since they could so easily topple over into sin. The language of war is so blunt that they could lose their feelings for the finer qualities of justice, truth, mercy and gentleness, and fail to see that Christian warfare is waged precisely through these qualities. When we speak of warfare we need to radically revise the content and meaning of our speech. Spiritual warfare has its analogies to actual battle, but it is essentially and profoundly different. The Bible makes these distinctions, and we shall trace how this is done. However, we must first gain some perspective on war as it appears in the Bible.

WAR IN THE BIBLE

A person who began reading the Bible at the beginning would quite quickly come up against the surprising fact that there is a great deal of war in the story of Israel. The most important issue in examining this theme is to trace not where it is at any given point but where it is moving toward. Yahweh, the God of Israel, is himself described unequivocally and centrally as a warrior, but the nature of this warriorship changes (Ex 15:3). Tremper Longman and Daniel Reid trace the war motif through various stages in the biblical revelation and demonstrate how it is modified as the story progresses.[2] Consider the following.

God fights for Israel. This is true in the period in which Israel is being established as a nation and in the tradition of holy war. Holy war is not like other forms of warfare.[3] It is undertaken not by human calculation but at the divine command; it is undertaken in human weakness and in dependence on God's promise; its aim is to reveal the fact that "the battle is the LORD's" (1 Sam 17:45-47). For this reason the stockpiling of weapons is *proscribed* (Josh 11:6) while immediate circumcision (not necessarily a wise military action!) is *prescribed* (Josh 5:1-3). After battle all plunder is to be offered up to the LORD in the "ban," devoted to God alone (Josh 6:24). The object of holy war is to demonstrate that God fights for his people and can be trusted. The glory belongs to him alone for the deliverance he brings. If pacifists have a hard time with the Old Testament so do adherents of just war theory. The Old Testament both proves too little and too much since what it advocates is neither approach but one other completely: holy war.

God fights against Israel. The suspicion that such a doctrine of war is convenient for Israel, allowing them to believe that their conquest of Canaan and the destruction of its peoples is legitimate, accords with the observation that all peoples create "national myths" to justify themselves. It is surprising then that the Hebrew Scriptures portray God turning against his own people because of their disobedience. National myths don't do this kind of thing. God gave them over to exile in Babylon as once they were in exile in Egypt. The exodus was reversed into exile. Yahweh became an enemy of his own people: "He has destroyed Israel" (Lam 2:5). Israel demonstrated here the ability to become self-critical and questioning of her own status. Out of this emerged a hope for a new act of deliverance from God and, in time, a vision of one "like a son of man" coming with the clouds of heaven (Dan 7:14 RSV).

The Lamb's war. For the Christian, the way in which holy war is redefined in the ministry of Christ is crucial. Jesus reinterprets the messianic expectation of a warrior-like deliverer. Military overtones are certainly there. The prophetic expectation of Malachi 4:5 points to the "great and terrible day of the LORD." Jesus is anointed as the Davidic Son (Mk 1:11). He faces an enemy (the devil) on his own ground (the desert) and prevails (Mk 1:12-13). He proclaims that the kingdom of God is at hand and casts out an evil spirit in the synagogue, so reclaiming holy space (Mk 1:14, 24). He gathers an army in the form of his disciples and gives them authority to "tread on snakes and scorpions and over all the power of the enemy" (Lk 12:17-20; military language if ever there was such). But then he enters into Jerusalem not on a war-horse but on a donkey (Mk 11:1-9). He trusts in God for victory in the tradition of holy war, but even more so, since he is not only weaker than his enemies but fully renounces the sword (Mt 26:47-56). He does not shed blood but has his blood shed while praying for those who take his life (Lk 23:34). In so doing he reinterprets holy war in the direction of nonviolence and self-sacrifice. This is the power that redeems.

Final victory. The biblical story looks toward final victory and does so using the image of the final battle of Armageddon in the most lurid terms (Rev 16:6). Yet it would be a mistake to believe that, having redeemed through the renunciation of violence in Christ, God then takes up the way of violence again to bring final resolution. Rather we are to see that in Christ (and in the book of Revelation) military language is subverted and reinterpreted to mean that the power at work in the cross in a Christ-like way is that same power that will finally overcome. In Revelation 5:5 the seer *hears* about the "Lion of the tribe of Judah" (traditionally a military image), but then immediately in Revelation 5:6 he *sees* "a Lamb standing as if it had been slaughtered." What he sees defines what he hears—that power we see at work in the Lamb of God is the power that will have the final victory in the conflict between good and evil.

That God's Word comes to us in Jesus Christ and the way in which he, in his actions, reinterprets and reapplies the theme of holy war is the norm for us. We may learn from the Old Testament traditions of holy war, but they can never now constitute for us a normative word but only a secondary one, as they bear witness to and are superseded by the Christ who is the Word of God. They may and should guide us as a metaphorical guide to spiritual struggle (1 Cor 10:6), but violence is no longer an option in serving the coming of God's kingdom in the name of Christ. With this background some important clarifications open up.

THE IDENTITY OF THE ENEMY

Paul finds it necessary to stress that the enemies of God are not flesh and blood individuals but the invisible powers that stand behind them (Eph 6:12). Our enemies are not mere flesh and blood (and therefore weak) but strong and threatening. We are to resist the temptation to see people as our enemies. This is difficult to do because, invisible though the powers of darkness must be, they exert their agency through people, some of whom may adopt a threatening posture toward the church. It is difficult not to respond to such provocation in like manner. Yet our spiritual struggle is not assisted by adopting the methods of those who oppose us. Once we regard others as our enemies then the battle is half lost. It is *for* people, not *against* people, that we wrestle with the invisible forces that enslave them and seek to enslave us. This is perfectly exemplified in the life of Jesus who drove out the prince of this world and yet treated his accusers, judges and crucifiers with compassion and respect.

Here we return to the "paranoid worldview." All of us, under pressure, resort to paranoid attitudes. We identify enemies and blame them for our misfortune. So we gain a degree of personal relief because we feel we have made sense of the situation. Paranoia pushes the blame onto others and enables us to feel relatively blameless. It is a psychological defense mechanism to preserve an inner sense of being in the right. When spiritual struggle leads to paranoia about individuals, or groups of individuals, we need to be wary. Paranoia and love cannot coexist. In naming the advocates (for instance) of Islam, or witchcraft, or spiritualism as "satanic," it becomes difficult to view those who are involved in these activities in any other way than as enemies. It erects a barrier that becomes difficult to cross, since fear and love do not easily dwell together. In denoting any of the structures of society as demonic we need to guard that we do not "demonize" those who are involved in them. In the first chapter we referred to the witchcraft crazes of former generations, a horrible example of this tendency.

We should take care that we do not make even more blatant mistakes. Walter Wink makes a perceptive comment on this. He points out that in the interaction between good and evil there are four "moments," or manifestations, which he indicates as follows:

1. God as God

2. God as "Satan"

3. Satan as "God"

4. Satan as Satan

Moments 1 and 4 are relatively unproblematic. These are the times when the activity of God or Satan is seen clearly for what it is. The complications come in 2 and 3 when the activity of God is perceived as that of Satan or that of Satan thought of as that of God.[4] According to Wink:

> A great deal that is creative or innovative is initially resisted as evil, and God's new creation is initially resisted as the work of the devil (God as "Satan"). When Jesus turned aside the current messianic role as satanic, and began to act on the basis of just those words that were proceeding from the mouth of God, the authorities declared him an enemy of God. When he cast out demons and declared this to be a sign of the inbreaking kingdom, he was accused of being in cahoots with Beelzebub.

So it is possible that what is truly of God is perceived as being satanic because it appears as something new and threatening. God's will for justice, mercy and truth may be seen as evil by the powers that be—the consequence being that Christians who are called to work for social transformation may even feel themselves to be stepping out beyond the pale of orthodoxy when they do so. In this way it becomes possible to understand the way in which some Christians oppose godly social change because even they perceive it as something threatening and satanic, while others, who perceive the rightness of such change, have their moral nerve paralyzed because they do not feel sure that what they think is God is not rationalized rebelliousness.[5]

To understand moment 3, Satan as "God," we must see that Satan can masquerade as God. Paul says as much when he speaks of Satan masquerading as an angel of light (2 Cor 11:14). That which actually belongs to Satan's activity can look and feel as if it is God's. Here we have the word of warning that is necessary when we begin to see others as enemies. It is the danger that we ourselves, in thinking that we are opposing Satan, may fall prey to satanic attitudes and become as much in the wrong as that which we are resisting. This is what happens when Christians become rigidly legalistic or morally slack. When we are hostile toward those who are different, or project evil onto others whom we regard as demonic, and believe that we are doing God's will, we could ourselves be becoming satanic. Yet such attitudes masquerade as moral rectitude and concern, for instance, for "biblical values."

People are not our enemies, and we should not treat them so. To do so drives out the possibility of responding to them with the love and compassion of Christ. The true enemies are the spiritual powers that are *beyond* people, and we too are prone to adopt satanic attitudes. This is why Jesus rebuked Peter moments after he confessed him as Messiah (Mk 8:33). Satan is equally willing to "suit up for either team."[6] He is equally willing to stir up opposition to the church or to stir up wrong attitudes within it. Simplistic black and white scenarios that see the church on one side as the faultless community and others as the corrupt enemy lead to the demonizing of opponents and the failure to love our enemies. The history of the church proves the case. We need only refer to the Crusades to get the point. We need to recognize the shadow across our own lives and the nuances of satanic activity, in addition to being self-aware.

THE WEAPONS WE USE

In the spiritual struggle we must also qualify the nature of our weaponry. According to Paul, "the weapons of our warfare are not merely human" (2 Cor 10:4). The spiritual conflict is fought on a spiritual level, not with physical or psychological weapons. We should engage the right "enemy" and do so in the right way and with the right weapons.

Here we dwell on the title of this chapter. The church faces a choice between the love of power and the power of love. Inevitably when the warfare image is deployed we begin to speak about power. The church must beware that in the struggle for society we are not struggling to maintain the powerful position that we have traditionally occupied. Part of what has called forth a more militant Christianity in recent years is not concern for the kingdom of God but the fear that we are losing control and not getting our own way. But when we play the world at its own game of being hungry for power, for cultural dominance, have we not already lost the battle? Power corrupts. A symptom of its corruption is that we find ourselves using the world's weapons. When Christians, or their organizations, bend the truth, massage statistics, use sensational headlines, deal in rumors, despise their enemies, behave aggressively, use the levers of power to their own advantage, they are behaving no differently from the rest.

Christian faith and worldly power do not mix, and when fused, faith becomes corrupted. If we think that spiritual warfare is about the ability of Christians to dominate the institutional life of society and compel conformity to a supposedly Christian ethic we are mistaken. History plainly shows that, however well intentioned, the attempt by the church to back righteousness with coercive power distorts the gospel. This does not mean that there is no place for the enforcement of law. It does mean that the role of the church is to argue and persuade to produce a consensus that may then be translated into voluntarily accepted legislation, rather than to use the remnants of its past power to impose legislation on a largely unwilling population. Such power as the church has must be "influence with" rather than "power over."

When the church has become a coercive force attempting to impose its own version of the moral code it has strayed a long way from Christ. Historian Ramsey MacMullen described how and by what means the early church grew within the Roman Empire.[7] Within two centuries the

174

church grew to be "all but in a majority" in many cities in the Empire. From A.D. 100 it grew by half a million in every generation until, by A.D. 312, there were five million Christians comprising one twelfth of the total population. In A.D. 313 the Edict of Milan promulgated by Emperor Constantine legalized the Christian religion and gave it official status. From A.D. 312-380 there followed what MacMullen calls the "Period of Flattery" when inducements were offered by the state for people to become Christians. This was followed by the "Period of Battery" between A.D. 380-390 with the attempt to coerce people to enter the church. Church growth during these latter two periods was very rapid, yet the kind of Christianity produced was corrupt, based as it was on flattery or battery.

The conclusion to be drawn is that the alliance of the church with the state that followed the Edict of Milan was probably the worst thing that happened to the church. It took it away from being a persecuted minority to being a persecuting majority. We are still seeking to recover from this. We should see significance in the fact that the turning point came for the church in A.D. 312, when Constantine won the battle at Milvian Bridge, which led to his becoming emperor. Before the battle, Constantine had a vision that showed him what he must do to defeat his enemies. As told by Constantine to the historian Eusebius, as he was praying he had a vision of a cross of light in the heavens bearing the inscription "Conquer by this." He was commanded to make a likeness of it to use in engaging his enemies. The likeness was the chi-rho monogram still used as a Christian symbol.[8] Constantine was inspired by a distortion of the battle imagery that is part of Christian vocabulary. The battle was interpreted as a physical one in which the weapons are far from being spiritual. This is an example of the danger of using the language of battle wrongly and then exploiting it for misdirected ends.

If not by worldly and coercive power, by which weapons should the spiritual struggle be waged? Here we refer to Jesus as our normative example. He refused the temptation to worldly power and came as neither a military nor a political messiah. He came healing the sick, liberating the oppressed and identifying with the poor and outcast. He was both respectful and critical toward the political and religious authorities. The upshot was that he died in weakness on a cross, sacrificing himself in love for enemies and friends alike. So he destroyed the hold of the devil, soaked up evil by his atoning death and gained the victory over death as proclaimed and revealed in his resurrection. By the power of gracious and forgiving love he disarmed the powers and principalities. He overcame evil by good. He resisted the temptation to overcome hostility by meeting it with an opposite and equal hostility, which is the "automatic" reaction of sinful human beings. Instead, he met it with steadfast and unflinching love in accordance with his own teaching in the Sermon on the Mount: "Love your enemies and pray for those who persecute you, so that you may be children of your Father in heaven" (Mt 5:44-45).

This is further illustrated by the problematic saying of Matthew 5:39: "But I say to you, Do not resist an evildoer." On the face of it, this verse enjoins a passive attribute toward evildoers, allowing them to triumph. But it need not represent an absolute position of nonresistance so much as a response in the specific circumstances the chapter goes on to describe.[9] The Greek text could contain an instrumental dative that would require a translation such as "Do not resist *by means of evil.*" What is here commanded is not carelessness or nonresistance on matters of principle but the response of love to individuals who may insult or misuse us.[10] This reflects the behavior of Jesus who both denounced wrongdoing and behaved forgivingly to wrongdoers. Jesus shows how spiritual warfare is engaged in, not by hostility, aggression and the use of power, but by the power of love. This must be how the church goes about its task. What exactly this might mean we sketch in the last chapter.

THE BATTLE THAT IS WAGED

A third area where the Bible qualifies the language of war concerns *whose* battle is being waged. In the use of military metaphors in the songs of the church the point has not always been clear that the battle belongs to the Lord. Yet precisely this is the conviction that was at the heart of Israel's understanding of holy war (1 Sam 17:45-47; 2 Chron 20:13-17). It is not helpful for us to sing about how we are going to destroy the enemy and execute justice because this obscures the fact that the battle is God's rather than ours and has already been won.

Concentration on the Lord as the warrior is needed rather than on ourselves. The theme of the helplessness of the people of God in the face of the enemy is deeply rooted in the holy war tradition. It is not we who are a match for the enemy, but the Lord, and our eyes are on him (Ex 15:1-8; 2 Chron 20:21-26). The drift of the Old Testament teaching is not that the people of God should become strong in order to overcome, but that they should remain vulnerable in order that they would need to trust in God to protect them. Basic to the Old Testament witness is that Yahweh fought by means of miracle, not through the armies of his people: "it was not by your sword or your bow" (Josh 24:12). For this reason the primary agent in the holy war was not the warrior but the prophet who interpreted what God was doing.[11]

With this in mind it is striking that the kind of warfare envisaged in Ephesians 6:10-18 is defensive. The soldier of Christ is told to stand (vv. 11-14), to resist the onslaught of the devil, rather than to advance and take his territory. Here is a useful corrective. It is Christ who advances and Christians who are called to stand. This should caution Christians from having too exalted an idea of themselves in the conflict. We do not spearhead the advance of the kingdom. The kingdom of God is like the mustard seed or the yeast that mysteriously grows or ferments (Mt 13:31-33). The kingdom comes of itself. We may pray for its coming, may serve it and may even hasten it. But we cannot bring it. This is God's work. To have it otherwise puts too much emphasis on mortals, even militant Christian mortals, and not enough on God.

It is not necessary for Christians to bind the strongman as if he had not already been bound. If Christ is now the head of every rule and authority and has driven out the prince of this world, then it is somewhat presumptuous for Christians to bind the "spirits" of nations. They should rather pray for the nations and for the greater coming of the kingdom. Perhaps along the way there are subsidiary aspects of the works of darkness that need to be confronted and frustrated by a word of authority in the name of Christ. But the assumption that guides our behavior apart from these isolated moments is that Christ has bound the powers and is now making them a footstool for his feet. We should not try to fight a battle he has already won since this is to give unwarranted credibility to the defeated powers. We should rather pray that the kingdom may come in greater fullness. We live in the confident expectation of the revelation of Christ's victory and not in the frantic fear that unless we do something the powers will rampage unchecked. This attitude enables us to engage in the struggle that remains with a serene and strong faith in God's ultimate victory and not with a hag-ridden fear that it all depends on us.

A further cautionary word is appropriate. The kingdom of God will not come in its fullness until the Lord appears. Then the kingdoms of this world will become the kingdom of our God and of his Christ (Rev 11:15). Our task now is to prepare the way for that day. The role of Christians is not that of an occupying, invading army but of a subversive guerrilla force. Perfection will elude us in the here and now. If we aim at a fully Christianized society we will be disappointed. We are to subvert and weaken as best we are able the power of an alienated world and the forces at work within it. We are looking forward and preparing for the day when God will take full possession of his world.

How should we go about this task? The final chapter will point the way ahead in some detailed ways. The cross is the means by which evil is overcome. This means that Christ did something once for all that is redemptive: he made atonement. But it means more. The cross sets the pattern for the power of redemption. It is cross-like action, becoming like Christ in his death, that introduces redeeming power into a fallen world. Overall, it must be by imitating Christ—by using the weapons of self-giving love and compassion, by identifying with the outcast and the poor rather than the rich and powerful, and by refusing to continue the vicious cycle of human hostility and aggression—that Christian people serve the coming of Christ's kingdom.

CHAPTER TEN

GOD'S HOLY WAR

The church of Jesus Christ is the church militant. We are engaged in spiritual conflict and need to be equipped for this task. To be sure, the conflict is like no other form of battle and the weapons quite different from any other weapons. We must re-imagine our notions of warfare. Yet the analogy is valid. It would be a pity if embarrassment at the military language or misplaced political correctness were to deprive us of the challenge.

The apostle Paul was well acquainted with Roman soldiers. He spent a certain part of his life being guarded by them. He may even at times have been chained to one. Out of his knowledge of a soldier's equipment he wrote the description of spiritual armor that we have in Ephesians 6:13-18. Yet there is a significant difference between bodily and spiritual armor. The soldier's armor was something external that he put on and took off. The Christian's armor is what he or she actually is. It is his or her very being, the quality of the life that is lived. The Christian puts on the armor (Eph 6:13) in the same way that he or she "puts on" or is "clothed with" Christ (Rom 13:14; Gal 3:27). By being transformed by the Spirit into the likeness of Christ we are "clothed" with Christ. In the same way, by being inwardly changed, we become the kind of people who are able to engage in spiritual conflict. It is when we are marked by righteousness, truth, readiness to witness, faith, the redeemed life, knowledge of the Word of God and prayer that we have become soldiers in the spiritual sense. It is certain that to be so changed an act of will is required from us. We must decide that this is the way we will be. The armor of God is not something external we put on or take off at will. It is our very being as Christians.

Walter Wink is not a pacifist but leans as far as he can in that direction. Unlike pacifists, who find nothing moral or admirable in the art of war or in those who ready themselves to wage it, Wink confesses to his admiration for truly committed warriors. After a lengthy and planned conversation with "very high army brass" at the Pentagon he wrote:

> I had longed at the time for further occasions for such conversation, primarily in order to convert them to my position. I would still cherish an opportunity, but now I would hope to be able to appreciate more than before what it means for them to be warriors, to defend the nation, and to regard that as a vocation. Perhaps, too, if they sensed my respect, and could see in me a fellow warrior, they might not have to circle their wagons so tightly. And what a contribution to nonviolent struggles it would make if we could learn from them the discipline, the toughness, and the willingness to face death for a higher cause that characterize the soldier![1]

The New Testament in particular holds up the military metaphor as illuminating of Christian discipleship. Christians are to be good soldiers of Christ Jesus (2 Tim 2:3). This is all the more remarkable in that, emerging from a Jewish milieu, soldiers would surely have been associated by the first Christians with oppression. Apparently admirable qualities could also be discerned in the profession. Effective soldiers are single minded and focused, disciplined and well trained, strong and brave, used to taking action, obedient to their superiors, fit and active. Above all they are skilled at making war and need to remain in a state of readiness for action. This is a model for Christian believers in general and those who would lead among the people of God should show these qualities in an exemplary way.

What kind of church ought the militant church to be? How will it hasten the coming of the kingdom of God and the final defeat of the power of darkness? By way of summary of what has already been expressed in this book, the following points may help to bring things into focus.

A BELIEVING CHURCH

The church must know what is to bear the shield of faith. It must believe in God—Father, Son and Holy Spirit—and take God with absolute seriousness. The God who is revealed in Christ and of whom Scripture speaks is the God who is the source of our life. He is not a being on the margins of our existence. He is our existence. The whole of life belongs to this God in whom we find the integrating center of life. To believe in God means to be fully persuaded in our minds that he is the one revealed in Christ, to be committed in our will and our affections to knowing and loving him, and to be occupied in our imagination and thoughts with God's vision. We have argued, and argue here again, that to believe in God means we radically *disbelieve* in the power of darkness. This does not mean that we think it is an illusion. We are mindful of its reality. But belief in God means that we reject the power of darkness. We refuse to be drawn to it or mastered by it. We treat it with scorn as that which has been mastered and overcome by the living God in Christ. We refuse to give it attention or glory. We are not impressed by it but see it for the whipped cur that it is. God is the source of our life and we are nourished by contemplating his beauty and knowing his joy.

A THINKING CHURCH

Perhaps no challenge is as important for contemporary churches than that of teaching people to think. Christianity is a thinking religion. In large measure the renewal movements of recent years in the church have been about the reclaiming of the intuitive and unconscious dimensions of human beings. In reaction to a perceived overintellectual, cerebral Christianity, they have stressed intuitive, immediate awareness of the Spirit of God. They have argued for the suprarational and the supranormal in Christian experience, for miracle and immediacy. These are well evidenced in the life of Jesus, the early church and the spirituality of God's people throughout the ages. This is a welcome corrective and a valid reclaiming of the breadth of experience for God. But we throw the baby out with the bath water if we teach people to devalue the quality of analytical, reflective thought to provide the counterpoint to mystical experience. The evidence is not that Christians think too much but too little. Without commitment to thinking as a basic Christian discipline we are liable to lapse into superstition and irrationality. The result will be that we will interpret wrongly our intuitive and mystical experiences and become prey to the dark power masquerading as an angel of light.

Theology is the church thinking through its faith, and Christians must give themselves to this task. Truth is part of our armor. The best way to counteract lies is to expose them with the truth. Enthusiasm, assertiveness and the will to believe are no substitute for clarity and persuasiveness of argument. If it is true that the devil is the father of lies (Jn 8:34), then speaking truth is part of the unmasking process. If it is true that Christians also are liable to be deceived (Lk 21:8) then we need, for our own sakes, to think carefully about the faith we profess in order that we may keep, and be kept, in the truth of Christ. In the history of the church it is clear that when Christians have been able to articulate their faith clearly and persuasively truth has tended to prevail over the lie.

A PROCLAIMING CHURCH

The Word of God is part of Christian weaponry. When the Word of God is preached in the power of the Spirit, a potent power is at work. The reason is clear enough. When it is preached, God himself is present in his Word. The events of the cross and resurrection become contemporary realities. From this a number of conclusions must be drawn.

First, it is a mistake to think of the spiritual struggle as a kind of esoteric, elitist activity that super-Christians engage in, which is a million miles away from what ordinarily happens when the church gathers. The reverse is the case. It is in the "ordinary" activities of the Christian community that spiritual warfare has its heart. As the Word of God is preached and expounded week by week there is spiritual engagement with the powers and a boundary of truth is established across which the power of darkness may not go. The power that rules through lies and deception is shown up to be what it is through the message of Christ crucified.

Second, for this to be the case, it must be the Word of God that is preached. Human opinions are not spiritually potent. Anecdotes and experiences may have their value in illustrating the preached Word, but they are not of themselves the Word of God. The renewing work of the Spirit of God is exercised through and by the exposition of the story, meaning and significance of Scripture. Therefore the proclaiming church must give attention to its own preaching in order that it may truly be the Word of God.

Third, the proclaiming church is misunderstood if the image that comes to mind is purely that of pulpits and pews. The Word of God is expounded in the community of faith, it is true. But preaching is more than this. To train preachers to be good pulpit performers can be misleading and incestuous if they are not also taught to engage the world in their proclamation. In the New Testament, pulpits did not exist. The vast majority of sermons there recorded were not preached in the church but in the world. Preaching is not pulpiteering. It is the total activity of the church in its verbal communication of the gospel emanating out of a community that places hearing that Word at its center.

A PRAYING CHURCH

As with preaching, praying is part of the very essence of the church and is itself, wherever and whenever it is found, part of our spiritual struggle. Paul tells the church at Ephesus to "pray in the Spirit at all times in every prayer and supplication" (Eph 6:18). Recently the custom has developed in the church of praying *against* things. Whatever the justification of this may be, and it is not well represented in the New Testament, our first responsibility is to pray *for* the world. This means putting ourselves in the role of the sympathetic participant in the drama of human affairs and, on the basis of the love of God for all, praying for community, nation and world.

When we pray, something happens in the invisible realm that undergirds and affects the visible realm. We should confess immediately that prayer is a mystery. It can only be understood if we presuppose that human history does not have the nature of a predetermined outworking of fate but of an interactive dialogue between God and humanity. In this interaction the process of history is formed and the world moves toward its ultimate goal. When Christians pray, they engage in the divine-human interaction and are involved with God on behalf of the human family in the coming of God's kingdom. In prayer it is as if God is given access into human affairs. When the Word became flesh, he came into a circle of devout praying individuals and families (Mt 1:18-25; Lk 1:6). In the same way, through the prayers of his people, the God who holds all things together gains greater access to the life of estranged and resistant humanity. It is very much the case that the prayers of God's people will serve the activity of the Holy Spirit in the world and will act as a boundary to that of evil. No doubt this is why Jesus taught his disciples to pray "Your kingdom come, your will be done, on earth as it is in heaven."

A LOVING CHURCH

We have gone to some pains to argue that, at this point in particular, spiritual warfare must be carefully understood. War is not naturally identifiable with love unless it is seen that we are fighting for people and not against them. The danger is that those who take the warfare seriously adopt inappropriately aggressive and militant attitudes that drive out the loving-kindness that we see in Jesus. How can Christians, for instance, resist the practice of homosexuality (presuming that they wish to do so) without at the same time alienating homosexuals and projecting an attitude of rejection toward them? We must face the fact that what we feel to be righteous indignation can communicate itself as persecution. Frequently the church finds itself on the horns of a dilemma here. The demands of moral theology compel the church to condemn sin. The demands of pastoral theology compel the church to love sinners. When the church condemns sin she is accused of not caring for sinners. When she cares for sinners she is accused of being soft on sin!

How do we get it right? Jesus had a striking ability to combine a clear call for righteousness with a great love for sinners. This is seen most clearly in the narrative of the woman taken in adultery (Jn 8:1-11).[2] The Pharisees were clearly using the woman's situation to trap Jesus and he appeared to be faced with the choice either of joining in their censorious and judgmental attitudes or of rejecting the teaching of the Old Testament on adultery. In this event, he neither allows himself to be drawn into their attitudes, thereby treating the woman as a nonperson, nor into condoning her sin. By treating the woman as a person and showing compassion to her, he gives her every incentive to leave behind her sin. When Christians in the name of morality give way to moralistic and judgmental attitudes that lose sight of individuals, they run the risk of being like the Pharisees from whom Jesus so clearly distanced himself. We do well to imitate Jesus in projecting a love for individuals that accepts them as they are and refuses to strike a condemnatory pose, while at the same time being shot through with a strong and pure morality that has no doubt that the well-being of each individual lies along the pathway of moral living. When it came to dealing with the powerless and victimized, Jesus demonstrated this attitude consistently. When it came to the powerful, he showed himself to be strong and forthright in condemnation.

A DISCERNING CHURCH

There is more to the gift of discernment than suspicion. The latter quality is regrettably in far greater supply than the former. We are all good at concocting conspiracy theories, and Christian attitudes toward the demonic can be wrongly determined by this. Because something happens that does not quite fit our plan, it does not necessarily mean that there is demonic interference. Frequently people excuse themselves from failure in relationships by saying, euphemistically, that "the enemy got in." There are those who tenaciously refuse to accept the truth about their own weaknesses of character or behavior by construing criticism as a satanic attack. Such language uses the devil as a convenient dustbin in which to dump garbage. He is a cipher for externalizing failure and sin. By projecting sin onto the external screen of the devil, responsibility is avoided. My point is that this is not discernment. It is symbolic speech that betrays a mental attitude. There is too much of it around. It functions as a "sorting myth" whereby we feel we have bottomed a situation by reference to a basic motif. Actually, we may be deceiving ourselves. There are times when the devil should be left out of things since the truth of a situation is obscured and not clarified by resort to such a thought.

A discerning church does not "think devil." It ignores the devil most of the time and perceives him to work only where he actually does. Just as we need extreme care before denoting a pastoral situation "demonic" so in the life of church and community such a diagnosis should only be put forward where it is genuinely appropriate. The church should be healthily skeptical of pseudo-spiritual language and yet truly discerning, attuned by the Spirit of God and the Word of God to discern the spirits.

AN AUTHORITATIVE CHURCH

What do we do when we discern the work of the devil in a given situation? We are not left defenseless. The church does not have in its armory the kind of coercive power that the world uses. Yet it is powerful with a different power, in that it is not power over people to oppress or control them but a power over the forces of evil to banish and frustrate them. This power liberates. It is rooted in the authority of Jesus, of whom it is recorded "he cast out the spirits with a word" (Mt 8:16) and "with authority and power he commands the evil spirits and out they come!" (Lk 4:36). Although in this book I have argued that the incidence of demonic activity is much less than some others would claim, there are occasions when it is the only diagnosis that will do. At such times the church should use its authority swiftly and appropriately.

Authority is vested in believers when they speak and operate in the name and by the Spirit of Jesus. This authority does not function outside of Christ and remains essentially *his* authority mediated from time to time through the believer and the believing community. So Jesus speaks to his disciples and says, "See, I have given you authority to tread on snakes and scorpions and over all the power of the enemy; and nothing will hurt you" (Lk 10:19). Through the Word, the power of the enemy is overcome. When the believer, having discerned such activity, speaks in the name of Jesus to overcome it, it is the presence and authority of Christ in that action and word that is the effective agent. This is not a magical power that functions at the believer's discretion but the authority of Christ active in the believer. This is where the gift of discernment is crucial. Using authoritative words without discernment risks treating the power of God as if it were something to be conjured up at will. To use such language as a matter of routine rather than one of discernment borders on the magic mentality.

A LISTENING CHURCH

A concern to emerge in this book is not to use the language of spiritual battle to produce or to excuse wrong attitudes toward those whom we might consider enemies. This has been described as the paranoid mentality. Not infrequently, wrong behavior is justified in spiritual terms. In failing to consult people or failing to behave courteously over a course of action, it is sometimes considered sufficient excuse that "the Lord told me to do it." The sense of spiritual conviction, however, should never be seen as a substitute for decent behavior. It creates a cynicism about spiritual things. It brings disrepute on the fact that there are times when God does indeed tell us to do things. That we are engaged in spiritual warfare does not excuse us from listening to others, even those with whom we disagree. When we listen with respect, sincerity and love we can more truly perceive what the spiritual issues are and where the battlefield really lies.

Wise words were spoken in this area by the Jewish philosopher Martin Buber (1878-1965). He argued that humankind knows two kinds of attitudes. There is the I-It attitude that marks our attitude toward the inanimate world. We relate to it as a thing and know it as such. The other is the I-Thou attitude in which we know God and others through personal relationships. We cannot know God or others through I-It attitudes. Buber goes on to say that, in what Christians would call evangelism, we need to develop I-Thou relationships of love and appreciative understandings of others, not the I-It approach that seeks to make proselytes by confrontation and loses sight of the fact that we are dealing with people.[3]

This is relevant to the militant church. In being militant it is necessary to stress that we are called to be lovingly militant and to achieve that same remarkable blend of discerning and authoritative opposition to evil combined with gracious and accepting openness to people that we see in the life of Jesus. We cannot truly love people without taking time to understand them and their ideas. To engage in dialogue with others, whether Marxist, humanist, Muslim, pagan or any of a dozen other ideologies, does not mean that we lessen our own convictions but that we accept others as made in the image of God.

AN ENGAGED CHURCH

If it is true that the "powers" are to be understood as both social and spiritual realities, there is an important corollary. Changing the world takes both social and spiritual resources. Social engagement and prayerful presence are equally necessary if the real world is to be engaged and changed. For this reason the Christian congregation exercises a strategic role within the wider society. Where two or three come together in the name of Christ there is a dynamic, an energy and a power that must be reckoned with. Jesus told his disciples that the kingdom of God was within them (Lk 17:21). Within and among Christian people there is a divine presence, one of which they may not be mainly conscious of, that works itself out in the world and makes a difference in it. For it to have impact Christians need to be engaged with the world around them, both in their spheres of work and service and in the shaping of societies and communities. This engagement is expressed through action and prayer as a dual strategy for transformation.

A FREE CHURCH

The final quality that we mention is that we be a free people. We cannot cooperate with God in freeing the world of the power of darkness unless we ourselves know that freedom. To be sure, final and complete freedom awaits the consummation. We will struggle with the darkness until the day when Christ brings the whole creation into its ultimate liberty. Personal temptations and sometimes failure will accompany the life of God's people until the coming of the Lord. There is no room for the spirit of self-confident triumphalism. We are not free of the shadow. But into today there has come the liberating power of tomorrow, which affords a foretaste of a glorious future. We have been set free from the power of the evil one to serve the living God. This is manifested in the freedom we have to worship and serve God, laying aside the old works of darkness in favor of pure and holy living.

If the spiritual authority of the church is lacking it is linked with the unwillingness of those who have been set free to live in freedom. While imprisoned by futile sins, uncaring, bigoted and un-Christian attitudes, and by conformist, worldly behavior, we lessen our effectiveness for God. It is truly free people who will serve God's purpose of liberation most effectively. Such living is what the devil now seeks to thwart. There is a battlefield in our hearts and in the church. This battle needs to be won for the sake of the wider battle in the world. Christ will never be the light of the world unless he is the light of the church. Yet even here, a strategy of darkness is to discourage us. When we see failure in the church we are tempted to despair. Even this discouragement must be refused as we confess that the church belongs to Jesus Christ and he is working his purpose out. The signs of Christ's victory are all around us. They can be seen in the conversions that take place daily, in the healing of lives and homes, in the faithful and sacrificial service of millions of Christians, in the renewing of old churches and the planting of new ones, the growth of trust and confidence, the thoughtful engagement with the world. There are indeed setbacks and failures, but Christ is building his church and the gates of hell will not prevail against it (Mt 16:18). Those who know this should bear it in mind. The time will soon dawn when Christ's victory will finally be revealed and the power of darkness will have had its day.

He who testifies to these things says, "Yes, I am coming soon" (Rev 22:20). Amen. Come, Lord Jesus.

NOTES

Preface

[1]Nigel G. Wright, *The Fair Face of Evil: Putting the Power of Darkness in its Place* (London: Marshall Pickering, 1989), published in the United States as *The Satan Syndrome: Putting the Power of Darkness in Its Place* (Grand Rapids: Zondervan, 1990).

[2]Walter Wink, *Engaging the Powers: Discernment and Resistance in a World of Domination* (Minneapolis: Fortress, 1992), p. 3.

[3]Gareth J. Medway, *Lure of the Sinister: The Unnatural History of Satanism* (New York: New York University Press, 2001).

[4]Ibid., p. 8.

Chapter One: The Satan Syndrome

[1]See on this Tim Tate, *Children for the Devil: Ritual Abuse and Satanic Crime* (London: Methuen, 1991), and Andrew Boyd, *Blasphemous Rumours* (London: Fount, 1991).

[2]Jean LaFontaine, *The Extent and Nature of Organised and Ritual Abuse* (London: Her Majesty's Stationery Office, 1994).

[3]Walter Brueggemann, *Theology of the Old Testament: Testimony, Dispute, Advocacy* (Minneapolis: Fortress, 1997), pp. 528-49. Brueggemann draws heavily on Jon Levenson, *Creation and the Persistence of Evil: The Jewish Doctrine of Divine Omnipotence* (San Francisco: Harper & Row, 1988).

[4]Origen *De Principiis* I/6.

[5]Mircea Eliade, ed., *The Encyclopaedia of Religion* (New York: Macmillan, 1987), 5:419.

[6]Walter Wink, *Unmasking the Powers: The Invisible Forces that Determine Human Existence* (Philadelphia: Fortress, 1986), p. 1.

[7]Morton Kelsey "The Mythology of Evil," *Journal of Religion and Health* 13 (1974): 16, quoted in Wink, *Unmasking the Powers*, p. 9.

[8]Rudolf Bultmann, in *Kerygma and Myth*, ed. H. W. Bartsch (London: SPCK, 1953), p. 5.

[9]D. E. H. Whiteley, *The Theology of St. Paul* (Oxford: Basil Blackwell, 1972), p. 19.

[10]*Kaleidoscope*, BBC Radio 4, April 25, 1985.

[11]I owe this phrase to Dr. Cyril Okeroche of Nigeria. It is an adaptation of the title of his article *"homo africanus is ipso facto homo religiosus."*

[12]Wink, *Unmasking the Powers*, p. 7.

[13]Emil Brunner, *The Christian Doctrine of Creation and Redemption* (London: Lutterworth, 1952), p. 135.

[14]Pennethorne Hughes, *Witchcraft* (Harmondsworth, U.K.: Penguin, 1965), p. 210.

[15]See for example: Michael Green, *I Believe in Satan's Downfall* (London: Hodder & Stoughton, 1981), pp. 112-26; John Richards, *But Deliver Us from Evil: An Introduction to the Demonic in Pastoral Care* (London: Darton, Longman & Todd, 1974), pp. 12-90; Michael Perry, *Deliverance: Psychic Disturbances and Occult Involvement* (London: SPCK, 1987), pp. 44-70.

[16]D. G. Brenner, ed., *Encyclopaedia of Psychology* (Grand Rapids: Baker, 1985), p. 795. See also Richard Broughton, *Parapsychology: The Controversial Science* (London: Ballantine, 1991); G. K. Zollschan, *Exploring the Paranormal: Perspectives on Belief and Experience* (Bridport, Dorset, U.K.: Prism Press, 1989).

[17]Perry, *Deliverance*, pp. 13-26.

[18]Ibid., p. 27ff.

[19]Ibid., p. 46.

[20]Ibid., pp. 55-59.

[21]Joanne Harris, *Chocolat* (London: Doubleday, 1999). See also David Burnett, *Dawning of the Pagan Moon: An Investigation into the Rise of Western Paganism* (Eastbourne, U.K.: MARC, 1991).

[22]Perry, *Deliverance*, pp. 61-63.

[23]I give a general overview in "Charismatic Interpretations of the Demonic," in *The Unseen World: Christian Reflections on Angels, Demons and the Heavenly Realm*, ed. Anthony N. S. Lane (Carlisle, U.K.: Paternoster Press, 1996), pp. 146-63.

[24]See John Allan, *Dealing with Darkness* (Edinburgh: Handsell Press, 1986), p. 1; Perry, *Deliverance*, p. 112; *The London Times*, March 26-27, 1975.

[25]*The Voice* no. 1012, May 20, 2002.

[26]*The London Times*, September 4, 1980; Perry, *Deliverance*, p. 112.

[27]*The London Times*, April 24, 1986; Perry, *Deliverance*, pp. 61-62.

[28]Is it accidental that two of the Christian bestsellers in recent years were the theologically disturbing novels by Frank Peretti, *This Present Darkness* (Westchester, Ill.: Crossway, 1986) and *Piercing the Darkness* (Westchester, Ill.: Crossway, 1989)?

[29]C. S. Lewis, *The Screwtape Letters* (London: Fount, 1942), p. 9.

Chapter Two: Disbelieving in the Devil

[1]Donald Guthrie, *New Testament Theology* (Downers Grove, Ill.: InterVarsity Press, 1981), p. 123.

[2]Ibid., p. 127.

[3]Michael Green, *I Believe in Satan's Downfall* (London: Hodder & Stoughton, 1981), p. 20. This statement is singled out for particular criticism in Edward Ball's review of the book in *Theological Renewal* 19 (1981): 33-36.

[4]Karl Barth, *Church Dogmatics* III/3, *The Doctrine of Creation: The Creator and His Creature*, trans. G. W. Bromiley and R. Ehrlich (Edinburgh: T & T Clark, 1960), p. 521.

[5]Otto Weber, *Foundations of Dogmatics* (Grand Rapids: Eerdmans, 1981), 1:489.

[6]Umberto Eco, *The Name of the Rose* (London: Picador, 1984).

[7]Andrew Walker, *Enemy Territory: The Christian Struggle for the Modern World* (London: Hodder & Stoughton, 1987), p. 10.

[8]The book is N. T. Wright, *Paul for Everyone: Galatians and Thessalonians* (London: SPCK, 2002), p. 105.

[9]Walter Wink, *Engaging the Powers: Discernment and Resistance in a World of Domination* (Minneapolis: Fortress, 1992), p. 34.

Chapter Three: Analyzing Evil I: Its Essence

[1]Lewis's position is summarized in Vernon R. Mallow, *The Demonic: A Selected Theological Study* (New York: New York University Press, 1983).

[2]Ibid., p. 219.

[3]Barth's discussion of this theme can be found in *Church Dogmatics* III/3, *The Doctrine of Creation: The Creator and His Creature*, trans. G. W. Bromiley and R. Ehrlich (Edinburgh: T & T Clark, 1960), pp. 289-368, 519-31. A useful summary may be found in John Hick, *Evil and the God of Love* (London: Macmillan, 1966), pp. 132-204.

[4]Karl Barth, *Church Dogmatics* IV/3, *The Doctrine of Reconciliation: Jesus Christ the True Witness*, trans. G. W. Bromiley (Edinburgh: T & T Clark, 1961), 1:178.

[5]Barth *Church Dogmatics* III/3, p. 289, particularly n. 1.

[6]Barth asserts in a significant "soundbite" that "das Nichtige ist nicht das Nichts" ("Nothingness is not nothing"). Ibid., p. 349.

[7]Ibid., p. 302.

[8]Ibid., p. 305.

[9]Ibid., p. 312.

[10]Barth *Church Dogmatics* IV/3, 1:177.

[11]Barth *Church Dogmatics* III/3, p. 531.

[12]Ibid.

[13]Ibid., p. 530, with reference to Is 14:12; Gen 6:1-14; Jude 6; 2 Pet 2:4.

[14]Ibid., p. 292.

[15]Ibid.

[16]Ibid., p. 349.

[17]Ibid., p. 519.

[18]Ibid., p. 416.

[19]Ibid., p. 457.

[20]Ibid., p. 450.

[21]Ibid., p. 579.

[22]Ibid., pp. 527-28.

[23]Ibid., p. 525.

[24]Ibid., p. 520.

[25]Ibid., pp. 351-52.

[26]Ibid.

[27]Karl Barth, *Church Dogmatics* III/1, *The Doctrine of Creation: The Work of Creation*, trans. J. W. Edwards, O. Bussey and H. Knight (Edinburgh: T & T Clark, 1958), p. 108.

[28]Hick, *Evil and the God of Love*, p. 140, n. 2.

[29]Gerhard von Rad, *Genesis* (London: SCM Press, 1961), p. 51.

[30]G. C. Berkouwer, *The Triumph of Grace in the Theology of Karl Barth* (Grand Rapids: Eerdmans, 1956), p. 378.

[31]Helmut Thielicke, *Theological Ethics: Foundations*, vol. 1 (Grand Rapids: Eerdmans, 1979), p. 114.

[32]See Wink's trilogy on The Powers: *Naming the Powers: The Language of Power in the New Testament* (Philadelphia: Fortress, 1984); *Unmasking the Powers: The Invisible Forces That Determine Human Existence* (Philadelphia: Fortress, 1986); *Engaging the Powers: Discernment and Resistance in a World of Domination* (Minneapolis: Fortress, 1992). These works are distilled in *The Powers That Be: Theology for a New Millennium* (New York: Doubleday, 1998).

[33]Wink, *Naming the Powers*, p. 99.

[34]Ibid., p. 103.

[34]Ibid., p. 105.

[35]Ibid.

[36]Wink, *Unmasking the Powers*, p. 4.

[37]Ibid., p. 12; See 2 Sam 24:1; 1 Chron 21:1; Zech 3:1-5.

[38]Ibid.

[39]Ibid., p. 15, with reference to Lk 22:31-34; 1 Chron 5:1-5.

[40]Ibid., p. 19.

[41]Ibid., p. 23. See Mt 10:25; 13:19; Jn 12:31; Eph 2:2; 1 Cor 10:10; 2 Cor 4:4; 6:15.

[42]Ibid., p. 24.

[43]Ibid., p. 25.

[44]Wink, *Unmasking the Powers*, p. 21.

[45]Ibid., p. 22.

[46]Jürgen Moltmann, *God in Creation: An Ecological Doctrine of Creation* (London: SCM Press, 1985), pp. 86-87.

[47]Ibid., p. 87.

[48]Ibid., p. 88.

[49]Ibid., p. 91.

[50]Ibid., p. 89.

[51]Alfredo Fierro, *The Militant Gospel: An Analysis of Contemporary Political Theologies* (London: SCM Press, 1977), pp. 171-72.

Chapter Four: Analyzing Evil II: Its Form

[1]Robert Cook, "Devils and Manticores: Plundering Jung for a Plausible Demonology," in *The Unseen World: Christian Reflections on Angels, Demons and the Heavenly Realm*, ed. Anthony N. S. Lane (Carlisle, U.K.: Paternoster Press, 1996), p. 180.

[2]Ibid., p. 181.

[3]Ibid., p. 182.

[4]Tom Noble, "The Spirit World: A Theological Approach," in *The Unseen World: Christian Reflections on Angels, Demons and the Heavenly Realm*, ed. Anthony N. S. Lane (Carlisle, U.K.: Paternoster Press, 1996), p. 220.

[5]Emil Brunner, *The Christian Doctrine of Creation and Redemption* (London: Lutterworth, 1952), pp. 107-8.

[6]D. E. H. Whiteley, *The Theology of St. Paul* (Oxford: Basil Blackwell, 1972), p. 19.

[7]Wesley Carr, *Angels and Principalities: The Background, Meaning and Development of the Pauline Phrase hai archai kai hai exousiai* (Cambridge: Cambridge University Press, 1981), pp. 175-76.

[8]John R. W. Stott, *God's New Society* (Downers Grove, Ill.: InterVarsity Press, 1979), pp. 267-75; Clinton E. Arnold, *Powers of Darkness* (Downers Grove, Ill.: InterVarsity Press, 1992).

[9]E.g., 1 Cor 2:8; Tit 3:1; Rom 8:38. See Green, *I Believe in Satan's Downfall* (London: Hodder & Stoughton, 1981), pp. 81-86.

[10]Hendrik Berkhof, *The Christian Faith: An Introduction to the Study of the Faith* (Grand Rapids: Eerdmans, 1979), pp. 208-9.

[11]A. B. Come, *An Introduction to Barth's Dogmatics for Preachers* (London: SCM Press, 1963), p. 220.

[12]John Macquarrie, *Principles of Christian Theology* (London: SCM Press, 1966), p. 241.

[13]Paul Tillich, *Systematic Theology* (London: Nisbet, 1968), 3:108-9.

[14]See also J. D. G. Dunn and Graham H. Twelftree, "Demon Possession and Exorcism in the New Testament," *Churchman* 94, no. 3 (1980): 222-23.

[15]Helmut Thielicke, *The Evangelical Faith: The Holy Spirit, The Church, Eschatology* (Grand Rapids: Eerdmans, 1982), 3:451.

[16]Brunner, *Christian Doctrine*, p. 139.

[17]Karl Barth, *Church Dogmatics* III/3, *The Doctrine of Creation: The Creator and His Creature,* trans. G. W. Bromiley and R. Ehrlich (Edinburgh: T & T Clark, 1960), p. 302.

[18]C. S. Lewis, *Mere Christianity* (London: Fount, 1952), p. 44.

[19]E.g., Ex 4:21; Rom 9:17; 1 Sam 16:14; Mt 18:7.

[20]John Calvin *Institutes of the Christian Religion* 3.23.8.

[21]Brunner, *Christian Doctrine,* p. 139.

[22]Tertullian *Apology* 22: "We are instructed, moreover, by our sacred books how from certain angels, who fell of their own free-will, there sprang a more wicked demon-brood, condemned of God along with the authors of their race, and that chief we have referred to. . . . Their great business is the ruin of mankind."

[23]Augustine *City of God* 11.11: "But there were some angels who turned away from this illumination, and so did not attain to the excellence of a life of bliss and wisdom."

[24]E.g., Karl Barth, *Church Dogmatics* II/2, *The Doctrine of God: The Election of God,* trans. G. W. Bromiley, J. C. Campbell, Ian Wilson, J. Strathearn McNab, H. Knight and R. A. Stewart (Edinburgh: T & T Clark, 1957), pp. 122-24.

[25]Brunner, *Christian Doctrine,* pp. 133-37.

[26]S. H. T. Page examines the relevant texts in *Powers of Evil: A Biblical Study of Satan and Demons* (Leicester, U.K.: Apollos, 1995) and comes to similarly cautious conclusions as those that follow.

[27]Green, *Satan's Downfall,* pp. 33-42 makes far too much of these verses.

[28]See on this Walther Eichrodt, *Ezekiel* (London: SCM Press, 1970), p. 392; John Mauchline, *Isaiah 1–39* (London: SCM Press, 1962), p. 140.

[29]J. N. D. Kelly, *The Epistles of Peter and of Jude* (London: A. & C. Black, 1969), p. 331.

[30]Brunner, *Christian Doctrine,* p. 139.

[31]Donald Bloesch, *Jesus Is Victor! Karl Barth's Doctrine of Salvation* (Nashville: Abingdon, 1976), p. 170.

[32]Barth, *Church Dogmatics* III/3, p. 481.

[33]E.g., Mt 13:39; Eph 6:11; 1 Pet 5:8; Rev 20:2.

[34]Lewis, *Mere Christianity,* pp. 46-47.

[35]Jn 12:31-33; Col 1:19-20; 2:15; 1 Jn 3:8.

[36]Oscar Cullmann, *Christ and Time: The Primitive Christian Conception of Time and History* (London: SCM Press, 1962), p. 198.

[37]Noble, "Spirit World," p. 205.

[38]Ibid., p. 215.

[39]Cook, "Devils and Manticores," p. 181.

[40]Job 26:12-13; Ps 74:12-14; Is 27:1. See also Rev 12:9.

[41]Reinhold Niebuhr, *The Nature and Destiny of Man: Human Nature* (New York: Charles Scribner's Sons, 1964), 1:178-244.

[42]Ibid., pp. 180-81, 254. Niebuhr is amazingly uncritical about the idea of the devil as a fallen angel.

[43]Ibid., p. 181.

[44]Noble, "Spirit World," p. 214, quoting Cook, "Devils and Manticores," p. 182.

[45]Walter Wink, *Unmasking the Powers: The Invisible Forces That Determine Human Existence* (Philadelphia: Fortress, 1986), pp. 24-25.

[46]Noble, "Spirit World," p. 215.

[47]Ibid., p. 216.

[48]Origen *De Principiis* 3.6.5: "For the destruction of the last enemy must be understood in this

way, not that its substance which was made by God shall perish, but that the hostile purpose and will which proceeded not from God but from itself will come to an end. It will be destroyed, therefore, not in the sense of ceasing to exist, but of being no longer an enemy and no longer death."

[49]Paul Ricoeur, *The Symbolism of Evil* (New York: Harper & Row, 1967), p. 260.

[50]C. S. Lewis, *The Screwtape Letters* (London: Fount, 1942), p. 114. I am grateful to Canon Tom Smail for reminding me of this incident.

[51]Noble, "Spirit World," p. 217.

[52]Ibid., p. 219.

[53]Ibid., p. 217.

[54]R. W. Jenson, *Systematic Theology: The Triune God* (Oxford: Oxford University Press, 1997), 1:117 n. 6.

Chapter Five: The Problem of Evil

[1]"World, world, O world! But that thy strange mutations make us hate thee." William Shakespeare, *The History of King Lear*, act 4, scene 1.

[2]Eli Wiesel, *Night* (Harmondsworth, U.K.: Penguin, 1981), p. 45.

[3]Ibid., p. 79.

[4]Norman Kemp Smith, ed., *Hume's Dialogues Concerning Natural Religion* (London and Edinburgh: Nelson, 1947), pp. 193-202.

[5]There is some discussion about the use of the term "metaphysical evil" with some commentators using it to refer to "the basic fact of finitude and limitation within the created universe." See John Hick, *Evil and the God of Love* (London: Fontana, 1966), p. 19.

[6]Quoted in Norman L. Geisler, *The Roots of Evil* (Grand Rapids: Eerdmans, 1978), p. 17.

[7]David F. Wright and B. Ferguson Sinclair, *New Dictionary of Theology* (Downers Grove, Ill.: InterVarsity Press, 1988), p. 381.

[8]John A. Sanford, *Evil: The Shadow Side of Reality* (New York: Crossroad, 1981), p. 10.

[9]Ibid., p. 9.

[10]Ibid., p. 55.

[11]J. W. Goethe, *Faust: Part One*, trans. Philip Wayne (Harmondsworth, U.K.: Penguin, 1949), p. 75.

[12]C. G. Jung, *Letters*, vol. 2 (Princeton, N.J.: Princeton University Press, 1975), p. 61, quoted in Sanford, *Evil: The Shadow Side of Reality*, p. 139.

[13]Sanford, *Evil: The Shadow Side of Reality*, p. 139.

[14]Alvin Plantinga, *God, Freedom and Evil* (Grand Rapids: Eerdmans, 1974), p. 54. This book is a cogent restatement of the free will defense.

[15]John Hick, *Philosophy of Religion* (Englewood Cliffs, N.J.: Prentice-Hall, 1973), p. 43.

[16]Hick, *Evil and the God of Love*, p. 92.

[17]Calvin *Institutes of the Christian Religion* 2.1.5.

[18]N. M. de S. Cameron, *Evolution and the Authority of the Bible* (Exeter, U.K.: Paternoster, 1983), pp. 70-71.

[19]Plantinga, *God, Freedom and Evil*, p. 58.

[20]Bruce Milne, *Know the Truth* (Downers Grove, Ill.: InterVarsity Press, 1982), p. 83.

[21]C. S. Lewis, *The Problem of Pain* (London: Fount, 1941), p. 123.

[22]Ibid., p. 124.

[23]I explore this in the chapter "Suffering," in *Christian Healing: What Can We Believe?* ed. Ernest Lucas (London: Lynx, 1997), pp. 109-39.

[24]N. P. Williams, *Ideas of the Fall and Original Sin: The Bampton Lectures for 1924* (London: Darton, Longman & Todd, 1927), p. 523 ff.

[25]Barth, *Church Dogmatics* III/3, *The Doctrine of Creation: The Creator and His Creature*, trans. G. W. Bromiley and R. Ehrlich (Edinburgh: T & T Clark, 1960), pp. 295-302.

[26]Ibid., III/3, p. 296, and also III/1, *The Doctrine of Creation: The Work of Creation*, trans. J. W. Edwards, O. Bussey and H. Knight (Edinburgh: T & T Clark, 1958), p. 377.

[27]Ibid., III/1, p. 320.

[28]Ibid., III/1, pp. 371-77.

[29]Ibid., III/3, p. 299.

[30]Martin Israel, *Exorcism: The Removal of Evil Influences* (London: SPCK, 1997), p. 42.

[31]Ibid., p. 44.

[32]Jürgen Moltmann, *The Way of Jesus Christ: Christology in Messianic Dimensions* (London: SCM Press, 1990), p. 303.

[33]Wiesel, *Night*, pp. 76-77.

Chapter Six: Inside Information?

[1]Arnold Bittlinger, *Gifts and Graces* (London: Hodder & Stoughton, 1967), pp. 45-46.

[2]See, e.g., Michael Harper, *Spiritual Warfare* (London: Hodder & Stoughton, 1970).

[3]Typical here has been C. Peter Wagner, *Territorial Spirits: Insights in Strategic-Level Warfare from Nineteen Christian Leaders* (Chichester, U.K.: Sovereign World, 1991). See also Roger T. Forster, *March for Jesus: History and Theology* (London: Ichthus Media Services, 1990).

[4]The words "demon possessed," although present in English versions, are used to translate the word *demonized,* which is found in various forms some thirteen times in the Gospels. See W. F. Moulton, A. S. Geden and H. K. Moulton, *Concordance to the Greek Testament* (Edinburgh: T & T Clark, 1978), p. 182.

[5]This report is now published as *Blumhardt's Battle,* trans. Frank S. Boshold (New York: Thomas E. Lowe, 1970). See also Douglas McBain, *Eyes That See* (Basingstoke, U.K.: Marshall Pickering, 1986), p. 60.

[6]Johann Christoph Blumhardt, *Blumhardt's Battle,* p. 18.

[7]Ibid., p. 55.

[8]Ibid., p. 56.

[9]Ibid., p. 57.

[10]James Bentley, "Christoph Blumhardt: Preacher of Hope," *Theology* 78 (1975): 578. Barth's use of the phrase can be traced in *Church Dogmatics* IV/3, *The Doctrine of Reconciliation: Jesus Christ the True Witness,* trans. G. W. Bromiley (Edinburgh: T & T Clark, 1961), 1:168ff. See also William Nicholls, *Systematic and Philosophical Theology* (Harmondsworth, U.K.: Pelican, 1969), p. 78.

[11]Eberhard Busch, *Karl Barth: His Life from Letters and Autobiographical Texts* (London: SCM Press, 1976), p. 43.

[12]Vernard Eller, *Thy Kingdom Come: A Blumhardt Reader* (Grand Rapids: Eerdmans, 1980), pp. xiv-xv.

[13]Karl Barth, *Theology and the Church* (London: SCM Press, 1962), p. 55.

[14]Johann Christoph Blumhardt, *Blumhardt's Battle,* p. 9.

[15]James Dixon Douglas, ed., *New International Dictionary of the Christian Church* (Exeter, U.K.: Paternoster, 1974), p. 851.

[16]Jessie Penn-Lewis with Evan Roberts, *War on the Saints* (New York: Thomas E. Lowe, 1973). This book was originally published in the 1920s. See also Eifion Evans, *The Welsh Revival of 1904* (London: Evangelical Press, 1969), pp. 168-74.

[17]Penn-Lewis, *War on the Saints*, p. 96.

[18]Ibid., pp. 54, 96.

[19]Ibid., p. 221.

[20]Frank and Ida Mae Hammond, *Pigs in the Parlor* (Kirkwood, Mo.: Impact, 1973), p. 12.

[21]Ibid., p. 16.

[22]Ibid., pp. 113-35.

[23]Ibid., pp. 123-33.

[24]Ibid., pp. 57-63.

[25]Ibid., pp. 59, 65.

[26]Ibid., p. 65.

[27]Ibid., p. 142.

[28]Bill Subritzky, *Demons Defeated* (Chichester, U.K.: Sovereign World, 1986), p. 2.

[29]Ibid., p. 12.

[30]Ibid., pp. 37-38.

[31]Ibid., pp. 67-82, 124-26.

[32]Ibid., pp. 208-9.

[33]Ibid., p. 212.

[34]Ibid., pp. 241-51.

[35]Subritzky's book in particular was influential in the founding of British-based Ellel Ministries whose director, Peter Horrobin, has developed his perspectives further in his own works *Healing Through Deliverance: The Biblical Basis* (Chichester, U.K.: Sovereign World, 1991) and *Healing Through Deliverance: The Practical Ministry* (Tonbridge, U.K.: Sovereign World, 1995).

[36]E.g., Don Basham, *Deliver Us From Evil* (London: Hodder & Stoughton, 1972).

[37]Particularly worthy of attention are the books by Kurt Koch, who was researching this area long before others: *Occult Bondage and Deliverance* (Berghausen, Germany: Evangelischer Verlag, n.d.); *Christian Counselling and Occultism* (Berghausen, Germany: Evangelischer Verlag, 1972).

[38]Don Cupitt, *Explorations in Theology*, vol. 6 (London: SCM Press, 1979), p. 50.

[39]For the development of this theme see Graham Twelftree, *Christ Triumphant* (London: Hodder & Stoughton, 1985), pp. 135-70; Graham Dow, "The Case for the Existence of Demons," *Churchman* 94, no. 3, pp. 199-208.

[40]See the international symposium edited by John Warwick Montgomery, *Demon Possession* (Minneapolis: Bethany Fellowship, 1976).

[41]Twelftree, *Christ Triumphant*, p. 120.

[42]Michael Perry, *Deliverance: Psychic Disturbances and Occult Involvement* (London: SPCK, 1987), p. 182.

[43]Dom Robert Petitpierre, ed., *Exorcism: The Findings of a Commission Convened by the Bishop of Exeter* (London: SPCK, 1972), p. 23.

[44]R. K. MacAll, "The Ministry of Deliverance," *Expository Times* 86 (1974-1975): 296.

[45]M. G. Barker, "Possession and the Occult—A Psychiatrist's View," *Churchman* 94, no. 3 (1980): 250.

[46]Perry, *Deliverance*, p. 82.

[47]Hammond, *Pigs in the Parlor*, p. 12.

[48]Ibid., p. 1.

[49]Barker, "Possession and the Occult," pp. 250-51.

[50]See further Twelftree, *Christ Triumphant*, p. 153ff.

[51]Gareth J. Medway, *Lure of the Sinister: The Unnatural History of Satanism* (New York: New York

University Press, 2001), p. 279.

[52]Jonathan Edwards, *The Religious Affections* (Edinburgh: Banner of Truth, 1961).

[53]See my article "Does Revival Deaden or Quicken the Church?: A Comparison of the Welsh Revival in 1904 and John Wimber in the 1980s and 1990s," in *On Revival: A Critical Examination*, ed. Andrew Walker and Kristin Aune (Carlisle, U.K.: Paternoster, 2003).

[54]In the foreword to Evans, *The Welsh Revival of 1904*, p. 6. It is also of great interest to discover Watchman Nee's spiritual and anthropological insights along the same lines in *The Latent Power of the Soul* (New York: Christian Fellowship, 1972).

[55]Perry, *Deliverance*, p. 48.

[56]See for a catalog of experiences C. D. B. Bryan, *Close Encounters of the Fourth Kind: Alien Abductions and UFOs—Witnesses and Scientists Report* (London: Weidenfeld & Nicolson, 1995). Medway makes a very strong case against the factualness of satanic ritual abuse in *Lure of the Sinister*, pp. 216-328: "In alleged cases of criminal Satanism, there are no missing persons, no bodies, no bones, no blood, no temples, no altars, no robes, no rituals, and no Satanists" (p. 329). He also sees evangelical Christians as the propagators of an unsubstantiated frenzy and is conducting his own kind of witch hunt against them.

[57]L. J. Suenens, *Renewal and the Powers of Darkness* (London: Darton, Longman & Todd, 1983), p. 95.

[58]Koch, *Christian Counselling and Occultism*, p. 218.

[59]Perry, *Deliverance*, pp. 82-97; Petitpierre, *Exorcism*, pp. 35-39; John Richards, *But Deliver Us from Evil: An Introduction to the Demonic in Pastoral Care* (London: Darton, Longman & Todd, 1974).

Chapter Seven: The Lordless Powers

[1]Andrew Walker, *Enemy Territory: The Christian Struggle for the Modern World* (London: Hodder & Stoughton, 1987), p. 35: "Evil may have intelligence, but the Devil's strategies against the church are not, it seems to me, to be understood as rational military strategies, rather they are more like desperate and increasingly vicious attacks."

[2]Kenneth Leech, *The Social God* (London: Sheldon Press, 1981), pp. 91-92.

[3]Ibid., p. 94.

[4]Ibid., pp. 95-96.

[5]Walter Wink, *Unmasking the Powers: The Invisible Forces That Determine Human Existence* (Philadelphia: Fortress, 1986), p. 39.

[6]Vernard Eller, *Thy Kingdom Come: A Blumhardt Reader* (Grand Rapids: Eerdmans, 1980), p. xix.

[7]Karl Barth, *Church Dogmatics* II/1, *The Doctrine of God: The Knowledge of God*, trans. T. H. L. Parker, W. B. Johnson, H. Knight and J. L. M. Hair (Edinburgh: T & T Clark, 1957), p. 633.

[8]Eller, *Thy Kingdom Come*, p. xx.

[9]Walker, *Enemy Territory*, p. 64.

[10]James S. Stewart, "On a Neglected Emphasis in New Testament Theology," *Scottish Journal of Theology* 4 (1951): 292-301.

[11]Ibid., p. 295.

[12]See also Jürgen Moltmann, *The Crucified God: The Cross of Christ as the Foundation and Criticism of Christian Theology* (London: SCM Press, 1974), pp. 128-35.

[13]Ibid., p. 136.

[14]There are the references in 1 Cor 10:20ff., but the point is accurate enough.

[15]Hendrik Berkhof, *Christ and the Powers* (Scottdale, Penn.: Herald Press, 1962).

[16]Rom 8:38ff.; 1 Cor 2:8; 15:24-26; Eph 1:20ff.; 2:1ff.; 3:10; 6:12; Col 1:16; 2:15.

[17]Berkhof, *Christ and the Powers*, p. 23.

[18]Ibid., p. 66.

[19]Ibid., p. 25: Compare the "all things" of Colossians 1:16 with that of 1:20.

[20]Ibid., p. 24.

[21]D. E. H. Whiteley, *The Theology of St. Paul* (Oxford: Basil Blackwell, 1972), pp. 20, 29.

[22]Walter Wink, *Naming the Powers: The Language of Power in the New Testament* (Philadelphia: Fortress, 1984), pp. 99-102.

[23]Ibid., pp. 104-5.

[24]John R. W. Stott, *The Message of Ephesians* (Downers Grove, Ill.: InterVarsity Press, 1979), pp. 260-87; and *The Cross of Christ* (Downers Grove, Ill.: InterVarsity Press, 1986), p. 233.

[25]Stott, *Message of Ephesians*, pp. 272-73.

[26]Ibid., p. 274.

[27]As is argued by Leech, *Social God*, p. 90.

[28]Whiteley, *Theology of St. Paul*, p. 29. See 2 Cor 6:15; Eph 4:27; 6:11.

[29]Michael Green, *I Believe in Satan's Downfall* (London: Hodder & Stoughton, 1981), p. 84. In reference to humans he cites Luke 12:11 and Acts 4:26, and to superhuman powers, Colossians 1:16; 2:15; Romans 8:38; Ephesians 6:12.

[30]Ibid., p. 86.

[31]Wink, *Naming the Powers*, p. 100.

[32]Markus Barth, *Ephesians 4—6: The Anchor Bible* (New York: Doubleday, 1976), p. 800.

[33]Stott, *Message of Ephesians*, p. 271.

[34]Green, *I Believe in Satan's Downfall*, p. 49.

[35]G. R. Beasley-Murray, *The Book of Revelation* (London: Oliphants, 1974), p. 191.

[36]I am grateful to my friend Graham Hooke of Lostock Hall, Preston, for transcribing the tape of this occasion, at which he was present.

[37]See the critique by Chuck Lowe, *Territorial Spirits and World Evangelization: A Biblical, Historical and Missiological Critique of Strategic-Level Warfare* (Fearn, Rosshire; and Sevenoaks, Kent, U.K.: Mentor/OMF, 1998).

Chapter Eight: De-demonizing Creation

[1]Floyd V. Filson, *The Gospel According to St. Matthew* (London: A. & C. Black, 1971), p. 150.

[2]G. R. Beasley-Murray, *Word Biblical Commentary 36: John* (Waco, Tex.: Word, 1987), p. 214.

[3]Peter O'Brien, *Word Biblical Commentary 44: Colossians, Philemon* (Waco, Tex.: Word, 1982), p. 129.

[4]J. N. D. Kelly, *The Epistles of Peter and Jude* (London: A. & C. Black, 1969), p. 163.

[5]Beasley-Murray, *The Book of Revelation*, p. 196.

[6]Gustaf Aulén, *Christus Victor: An Historical Study of the Three Main Types of the Atonement* (London: SPCK, 1931), p. 20.

[7]Ibid., pp. 20-21.

[8]Ibid., p. 83ff.

[9]Ibid., p. 32ff.

[10]Ibid., p. 124.

[11]Paul Althaus, *The Theology of Martin Luther* (Philadelphia: Fortress, 1966), p. 220.

[12]John R. W. Stott, *The Cross of Christ* (Downers Grove, Ill.: InterVarsity Press, 1986), pp. 231-39.

[13]Peter O'Brien, "Principalities and Powers: Opponents of the Church," in *Biblical Interpretation*

and the Church, ed. D. A. Carson (Exeter, U.K.: Paternoster, 1984), p. 138.

[14]Andrew Walker, Enemy Territory: The Christian Struggle for the Modern World (London: Hodder & Stoughton, 1987), p. 34.

[15]Karl Barth, Church Dogmatics IV/4, The Christian Life: Baptism as the Foundation of the Christian Life, trans. G. W. Bromiley (Edinburgh: T & T Clark, 1969), p. 228. The chapter headings "The Lordless Powers" and "De-demonizing Creation" are inspired by this section: pp. 213-32.

[16]Ibid., p. 216.

[17]Walter Wink, Engaging the Powers: Discernment and Resistance in a World of Domination (Minneapolis: Fortress, 1992), passim.

[18]Colin Gunton, "Christus Victor Revisited," Journal of Theological Studies 35 (April 1985): 142.

[19]Aulén, Christus Victor, p. 176.

Chapter Nine: The Love of Power and the Power of Love

[1]Karl Barth, Church Dogmatics III/4, The Doctrine of Creation: The Command of God the Creator, trans. A. T. Mackay, T. H. L. Parker, H. Knight, H. A. Kennedy and J. Marks (Edinburgh: T & T Clark, 1961), p. 454.

[2]Tremper Longman III and Daniel G. Reid, God Is a Warrior (Carlisle, U.K.: Paternoster Press, 1995). See also my article, "Preaching on 'Holy War,' " Preaching Today, Summer 2000, pp. 3-10.

[3]See Millard C. Lind, Yahweh Is a Warrior: The Theology of Warfare in Ancient Israel (Scottdale, Penn.: Herald Press, 1980).

[4]Walter Wink, Unmasking the Powers: The Invisible Forces That Determine Human Existence (Philadelphia: Fortress, 1986), p. 35.

[5]Ibid. See also Mk 3:22.

[6]Wink, Unmasking the Powers, p. 33.

[7]Ramsey MacMullen, Christianizing the Roman Empire: AD 100—400 (New Haven, Conn.: Yale University Press, 1984).

[8]K. S. Latourette, A History of the Expansion of Christianity: The First Five Centuries (Grand Rapids: Eerdmans, 1970), 1:158.

[9]David Hill, The Gospel of Matthew (London: Oliphants, 1972), p. 128.

[10]R. T. France, Matthew (Leicester, U.K.: Tyndale Press, 1985), p. 126.

[11]Lind, Yahweh Is a Warrior, p. 23.

Chapter Ten: God's Holy War

[1]Walter Wink, Engaging the Powers: Discernment and Resistance in a World of Domination (Minneapolis: Fortress, 1992), p. 291.

[2]It is debated of course whether this passage, which does not properly fit its given context, really belongs to the biblical canon. I make the assumption here that it does but am aware of the arguments against this.

[3]Martin Buber, I and Thou (Edinburgh: T & T Clark, 1958), and Between Man and Man (London: Kegan Paul, 1962), pp. 17-36.

Scripture Index